LENT WITH THE FATHERS

General Editors

✠ Maurice Couve de Murville, Archbishop of Birmingham
Fr David McLoughlin
Fr David Evans

Oscott College was founded near Birmingham in 1794 at a time when students and staff from the English Catholic colleges abroad were being driven home by the French Revolution. In 1838 it occupied new buildings at Sutton Coldfield, built in the Gothic style, in a move which inaugurated an ambitious phase of the Catholic Revival in England. Oscott is the seminary of the Archdiocese of Birmingham which also has students from many others dioceses.

The Oscott Series aims at continuing the role of Oscott as an intellectual and spiritual centre of English Catholicism for close on two hundred years.

Other titles in the series are:

LENT WITH THE FATHERS

Readings selected

and translated

by

BRUCE HARBERT

Oscott Series 8

VERITAS

First published 1994 by
Veritas Publications
7-8 Lower Abbey Street
Dublin 1

ISBN 1 85390 202 0

British Library Cataloguing
in Publication Data.
A catalogue record for
this book is available
from the British Library.

Cover design by Banahan McManus, Dublin
Printed in the Republic of Ireland
– by Colour Books Ltd., Dublin

CONTENTS

FOREWORD

In this book you will find a commentary on the Gospel for each day in Lent and Holy Week written by one of the Fathers of the Church. For the most part, the commentaries on Matthew's Gospel are by Saint John Chrysostom, those on Mark by Saint Bede the Venerable, those on Luke by Saint Ambrose and those on John by Saint Augustine.

The translation of Scripture used is the New Revised Standard Version, but because the Scripture text that the Fathers knew often differs from that now agreed on, the translations will sometimes be found to deviate from the NRSV. Moreover, sometimes the Fathers see in the biblical text a meaning that is genuinely there in the original, but cannot be gleaned from the NRSV or any other modern translation, and here again the NRSV has been altered. An example is John 8:24,[1] where *I am* is used instead of *I am he* to make the meaning of Augustine's comments clear.

This collection of texts is intended to help in the reading and interpretation of Holy Scripture *by the light of the Spirit who inspired its writing*[2] and *in the living Tradition of the whole Church*.[3] In approaching the Fathers' interpretation of Scripture, it is helpful to distinguish several kinds of meaning they find in the text.

First comes the *literal* sense,[4] of which Saint John Chrysostom is the master. He was educated at Antioch, where there had long been a flourishing school of scriptural scholarship principally concerned with discovering and explaining the literal meaning of the sacred text. An example of his approach is his analysis of Matthew's gospel of the Resurrection,[5] where he leads us by the hand from word to word, bringing to life the events narrated, and illuminating details that might easily be missed.

Three other kinds of interpretation are collectively known as *spiritual* or *mystical*. We shall give a brief description of these, with one or two examples in each case.[6]

7

The first is called *allegorical* (from a Greek word meaning 'to say something else'), and sees the literal meaning of the text as a sign of some doctrine or practice of the Christian faith. For instance, the Fathers, following Saint Paul, often see the passage of the Israelites through the Red Sea as a sign of Christ's passage through death to life, and of Christian baptism.[7] Ambrose takes the phrase *the finger of God* as his starting-point for a discussion of the doctrine of the Holy Trinity.[8]

The second kind of interpretation is *moral*. Saint John Chrysostom loves this as well, and tends to draw a moral lesson after his exploration of the literal meaning of the Gospel text. There are several examples of this in the earlier part of Lent, where Chrysostom comments on the Sermon on the Mount in Matthew's Gospel.[9] Ambrose explores the moral sense in his commentary on the parable of the Prodigal Son.[10]

Finally, *anagogical* interpretation (from a Greek word meaning 'to lead upwards') looks in the Scripture for signs of Christ's Second Coming, the establishment of God's kingdom, and our hope of glory. Bede, for example, finds such signs in the angels who attend Christ in the desert[11] and in the song of the crowd as he enters Jerusalem.[12]

Some of these interpretations will seem far-fetched to modern readers, especially perhaps the significance attached by the Fathers to numbers that occur in the Gospel text.[13] However, I have adopted a hospitable policy in my choice of texts in the hope that, while no reader is likely to find every one of these passages to his or her liking, many may find new friends and pleasant surprises.

Running through all the kinds of interpretation described above is a strong sense of the *unity* of Holy Scripture.[14] The Fathers saw the New Testament as the fulfilment of the Old, and as the key to its right interpretation. For an example, see Ambrose's explanation of the presence of Moses and Elijah at the Transfiguration of Christ.[15] This understanding inspires them to bring into conjunction texts from widely separate parts of the Bible in surprising and illuminating ways. They also juxtapose texts from different Gospels in ways that may seem uncritical to the eye of modern biblical scholarship, but witness to the unity of the Gospel message handed on to the Church by the four Evangelists, whom another Father images as four beasts drawing a single chariot on which Christ is enthroned.[16]

These texts should be read in close conjunction with the Gospel of the day, and with this in view an extract from the Gospel, long enough to make the accompanying patristic commentary intelligible, has often been printed at the head of the commentary. Sometimes, when the commentator is concerned to set the Gospel passage within a wider context, it may be helpful to read a whole chapter of the Gospel, not simply the extract appointed for the liturgy of the day.

Many of the writings on Scripture that have come down to us from the Fathers, including much that is in this book, began life in the form of sermons. They were presumably altered when written down to be read, but they still bear the marks of their origin. With Augustine and Chrysostom in particular, we can still hear the voice of the preacher straining to hold the attention of his audience.

The Fathers need to be read slowly and savoured. Some passages, particularly those by Saint Ambrose, are very concise and allusive. Medieval monks used to compare a Christian slowly and meditatively reading the Fathers to a cow chewing its cud.

For anybody who wishes to find these texts in the original, references are given to the *Patrologia Graeca (PG)* and *Patrologia Latina (PL)* of Migne.

Omissions are indicated by the sign <>. The Hebrew numbering is followed for the Psalms, in accordance with the practice of the NRSV.

Bruce Harbert
Saint Mary's College
Oscott
Ash Wednesday, 1993

9

NOTES

1. Week 5 Tuesday.
2. *Catechism of the Catholic Church* 111; Vatican Council II, *Constitution on Divine Revelation* 12.
3. *Catechism of the Catholic Church* 113.
4. *Catechism* 116.
5. Paschal Vigil Year A.
6. Cf. *Catechism* 117.
7. e.g. Augustine commenting on the Gospels of Sunday Week 3 Year B and Saturday Week 4.
8. Week 3 Thursday.
9. Ash Wednesday and Tuesday, Thursday, Friday and Saturday of Week 1.
10. Week 2 Saturday and Week 4 Sunday Year C.
11. Week 1 Sunday Year B.
12. Palm Sunday Year B (Gospel for the Procession).
13. e.g. Augustine on Tuesday of Week 4 or Ambrose on Tuesday of Week 2.
14. *Catechism* 112.
15. Sunday Week 2 Year C.
16. Irenaeus *Adversus Haereses* 3, 11, 8; *PG* 7, 886-887. Cf. Vatican Council II *Constitution on Divine Revelation* 18.

NOTES ON THE FATHERS

Saint Ambrose (c. 339-397) was born in Trier. He had a successful career as a Roman civil servant until he was called by popular acclaim to become Bishop of Milan (in 374) before he had even been baptized. He was a strong bishop, not afraid to stand up to the Emperor and his family, and a noted preacher. He wrote scriptural commentaries, moral and doctrinal treatises and hymns, all in Latin, although he could read Greek. He was largely responsible for the conversion of Saint Augustine, and baptized him.

Saint John Chrysostom (c. 347-407) lived his early life at Antioch, where he became a monk and was noted as a preacher and commentator on Scripture. There he delivered the sermons that were collected to form his commentary on the Gospel according to Matthew. He also wrote many other works on Scripture. All his writings are in Greek. In 398 he became Patriarch (Bishop) of the imperial city of Constantinople, but he met with opposition from the Imperial Family and was unjustly suspected of heresy. As a result, he was deposed from his see in 403 and died in exile.

Saint Augustine (354-430) was born at Tagaste in North Africa. He moved to Italy, followed a literary career and lived with a woman who bore him a son. In 387 he was baptized, and soon afterwards returned alone to Africa, where he was ordained priest, and in 396 became Bishop of Hippo. Much of his energy from then on was occupied with combating heterodox Christian teaching, and he produced a large body of writing on doctrinal subjects to this end. Letters, sermons and scriptural commentaries also survive among his voluminous writings, all of them in Latin. He knew no Greek. He wrote *The City of God* to give a Christian interpretation of the fall of Rome to barbarian invaders. His best-known work is his autobiography, the *Confessions*.

Saint Gregory the Great (c. 540-604) made a promising beginning of a civil career in Rome, but became a monk in the monastery of Saint Andrew in the city. The Pope used him as an envoy, and in 590 he was elected Pope himself. He was an effective administrator who greatly extended the influence of the Papacy. Among his writings many letters, sermons and scriptural commentaries survive, together with the *Pastoral Care*, a treatise on the office of a bishop. He wrote in Latin.

Saint Bede (c. 673-735) is often known as 'the Venerable Bede'. He spent almost all his life at Jarrow in North-East England as a monk, writing Latin historical works and scriptural commentaries. His historical writings form an invaluable and unique source for the early history of England, while his works on Scripture show an ingenious and original mind with a deep knowledge of the earlier Latin fathers.

1

ASH WEDNESDAY TO THE FIRST SATURDAY IN LENT

1. Ash Wednesday

Jesus said *Beware of practising your piety before others*, and then went on to add *in order to be seen by them*.[1] It sounds as though he said the same thing twice, but if you think about it carefully, they are not the same but two different things, and his words show great common sense, together with immeasurable care and sensitivity.

It is possible for us both to do things in the sight of others without wishing to be seen by them, and also to hide our deeds from them while we really wish them to notice. So it is not merely the external deed, but the thought behind it that Jesus singles out for blame or praise. Had he not spoken so carefully, this saying would have made many people hesitate about giving alms, since we cannot always and everywhere give alms secretly. And so, freeing us from the obligation of doing that, he fixes both our punishment and our reward, not according to the result of our deeds, but according to the intention we have when we do them. This is to prevent us from saying 'Why should I be penalised if somebody else sees what I do?' 'That is not what I am concerned about', says Jesus; 'I look at your thoughts, and at the way in which your deeds are done'. He desires to mould our souls, to heal them from all their sicknesses. So, having spoken against doing a thing for show, and having taught us that as a penalty for this our actions become vain and futile, he lifts up the minds of his hearers again by speaking of the Father and of heaven. He means not only to sting their consciences by speaking of punishment, but also to awaken their sense of reverence by speaking of the Father who gave them birth. <>

He wishes his hearers to understand that God is present everywhere, and that he has not limited our concerns to this present life, but that when we leave it we must come before a more terrible court of law where all our deeds will be accounted for, we shall be rewarded or punished, and no action will be hidden, small or large, even though it may seem to be concealed from human eyes. This is what he is hinting at with the words *Your Father who sees in secret will reward you*.[2] He brings his hearers before a great and distinguished audience, granting them in abundance the publicity they seek. 'What do you desire?' he asks, 'Are you not looking for spectators to see what you do? Well, here you have not angels or archangels, but the God of all'. And if you also wish to have human spectators, God will not deny you them at the proper time: he will give you them in much greater numbers. If you show off here, you can only do so in front of ten or twenty people, or perhaps a hundred; but if you take care to keep your deeds secret now, God himself will proclaim them in the sight of the whole universe. (Saint John Chrysostom)[3]

2. Thursday

Jesus warns his disciples not to tell anybody that *the Son of Man must undergo great suffering, and be rejected by the elders, chief priests, and scribes and be killed, and on the third day be raised*.[4] Perhaps the Lord added this because he knew that even the disciples would find it difficult to believe in his passion and resurrection. So he preferred to announce them himself, so that when they took place they might inspire faith, and that rumours about them might not cause discord. So Christ did not wish to boast, but preferred to seem inferior, and so to undergo his passion: and you, who were born inferior, do you boast? You must travel by the road that Christ walked. To do this is to know him, to imitate him, in good reputation and bad, that you may boast in the Cross, just as he has boasted. That was how Paul walked, and so he boasts, saying, *may I never boast of anything except the cross of our Lord Jesus Christ.*[5]

But let us see why it is that in Matthew's Gospel we find that the disciples are warned *not to tell anyone that he was the Christ,*[6] while here it is written that they were told not to tell anybody that he was to suffer much and to rise again.[7] It is because everything is contained in the name of Christ: he is the Christ who was born of the virgin, he is the Christ who worked miracles among the people, who died for our sins and rose from the dead. Take one of these away, and you have taken away your salvation. Heretics too seem to have their Christ, for none of them denies the name of Christ; but whoever fails to acknowledge anything that belongs to Christ is thereby denying Christ himself. There are many reasons why he commands his disciples to be silent: to deceive the prince of the world, to avoid boasting, to teach humility, and so that his disciples, still weak and imperfect as they are, may not be oppressed by the weight of the full and mighty preaching of the gospel.

The apostles are forbidden to tell anyone the good news that he is the Christ, the Son of God, so that later on they may proclaim the good news of the Cross. The only reason that you, as one of the faithful, have to boast, is that you truly understand the Cross of Christ. No other crosses are worth anything to me, but the only one that has true value is Christ's Cross, *by which the world has been crucified to me, and I to the world.*[8] If the world has been crucified to me, I know that it is dead, and I do not love it or desire it: I know that this world is being consumed by corruption, and I avoid it as something rotten, I beware of it as something unclean, I leave it, for otherwise it will do me harm. (Saint Ambrose)[9]

3. Friday
Why do we and the Pharisees fast often, but your disciples do not fast?[10] Here we see the disease that Christ was rooting out some time ago when he said *when you fast, put oil on your*

head and wash your face,[11] knowing in advance the evils that spring from that disease.

He does not rebuke these men or call them 'you arrogant busybodies', but speaks to them with all kindness, saying *The wedding guests cannot mourn as long as the bridegroom is with them, can they?*[12] When he was speaking up for other people – I mean the tax-collectors – he spoke more harshly to those who were criticising them, in order to soothe their wounded souls; but when it is he and his disciples who are being mocked, his response is gentle. <>

Earlier, he spoke of himself as a physician,[13] and now he calls himself the bridegroom: through these names he reveals inexpressible mysteries. He might have spoken more aggressively, and said, 'You are not masters of these things. You have no right to lay down the law in this way! What is the value of fasting, when your mind is full of wickedness, when you accuse others, when you condemn them, carrying about beams in your eyes,[14] and do everything for display? Before all these things you should have thrown out pride, and acquired all the other virtues, charity, gentleness, brotherly love.' But he says nothing like this: rather, with all gentleness, *The wedding guests cannot mourn as long as the bridegroom is with them, can they?*[15] reminding them of the words of John, who said *He who has the bride is the bridegroom; the friend of the bridegroom, who stands and hears him, rejoices greatly at the bridegroom's voice.*[16] What he is saying is something like this: the present time is one of joy and happiness, so do not bring in a note of gloom. Fasting is depressing, not by its nature, but for those who are still weak: to those who at least wish to live religiously it is very sweet and desirable. Just as when we enjoy bodily health we are very cheerful, so when our soul is well, our pleasure is even greater. (Saint John Chrysostom)[17]

4. Saturday

After this he went out and saw a tax collector named Levi, sitting at the tax booth; and he said to him, 'Follow me.'

And he got up, left everything, and followed him. Then Levi gave a great banquet for him in his house; and there was a large crowd of tax collectors and others sitting at the table with them.[18]

We come now to the mystery of the calling of the publican, whom Jesus commands to follow him, not with bodily steps, but with the affection of his mind. So a man who before, in his greed for gain, made a cruel living from what fishermen had managed to earn by the labours and dangers of their hard lives, hears the Word calling him with a single word, leaves behind his possessions – he who used to steal other people's possessions – and abandoning that vile place follows after the Lord with total commitment. Next, he reveals the great banquet that he has prepared: for whoever receives Christ into his inner dwelling feeds on the greatest delicacies of overflowing pleasures. Therefore the Lord comes in gladly and reclines in the love of one who has believed.

But again the envy of the treacherous flares up, and we see a sign of future punishment, for while the faithful are feasting and reclining in the kingdom of heaven, traitors will be punished with fasting. We can also see here the difference between the followers of the Law and of grace: those who follow the Law will suffer the eternal hunger of a mind deprived of nourishment, while those who have received the word deep within their souls will be refreshed with heavenly nourishment and an overflowing fountain, so that they know neither hunger nor thirst. That is why those who were spiritually famished complained and asked *Why does he eat and drink with publicans and sinners?*[19] That is the voice of the serpent, whose first words to Eve were *Did God say 'You shall not eat from any tree?'*[20] Thus they are spreading their father's poison who say: *Why does he eat and drink with publicans and sinners?* By eating with sinners, the Lord allows us to feast even with the Gentiles, saying: *Those who are well have no need of a physician, but those who are sick.*[21]

Our new teacher has brought us a new medicine which has not grown up out of the earth: no creature knows the secret of this remedy. Come, all who have fallen into various diseases of sin, make use of this new remedy, brought from a far country, by which the poison of the serpent is warded off. It has removed not only the scar of our suffering, but also the cause of our dreadful wound. This is a medicine that does not require fasting but gives food to the soul, for the Son of Man came eating and drinking, and they say 'he has a demon',[22] and our minds are not starved of divine nourishment. The people who are fasting are those from whom Christ is absent, who lack abundance of good works. A person who finds in a virtuous life enough pleasure to satisfy his desire and who receives Christ into his house reveals a great banquet, that is, a spiritual feast of good works, a meal where the rich go without while the poor have plenty. And therefore, he says You cannot make wedding guests fast while the bridegroom is with them.[23] (Saint Ambrose)[24]

NOTES

1. Matt 6:1
2. Matt 6:4
3. *Commentary on Matthew* 19,1-2; *PG* 57, 274-275
4. Luke 9:22
5. Gal 6:14
6. Matt 16:20
7. Luke 9:21-22
8. Gal 6:14
9. *Commentary on Luke* 6,100-101; *PL* 15,1782.
10. Matt 9:14
11. Matt 6:17
12. Matt 9:15
13. Matt 9:12
14. Matt 7:3
15. Matt 9:15

16. John 3:29
17. *Commentary on Matthew* 30, 3; *PG* 57, 366.
18. Luke 5:27-29
19. Mark 2:16; cf. Luke 5:30
20. Gen 3:1
21. Luke 5:31
22. cf. Luke 7:34
23. Luke 5:34
24. *Commentary on Luke* 5,16-19; *PL* 15,1724-1725

2

THE FIRST WEEK OF LENT

1. Sunday Year A

If you are the Son of God, command these stones to become loaves of bread.[1]

He does not say 'since you are hungry', but *if you are the Son of God*, seeking to deceive Jesus with flattery. The Devil did not mention hunger, because he did not want to seem to be taunting Jesus by drawing attention to it. Being ignorant of the greatness of God's plan, he thought Jesus would be ashamed of being hungry, and so, with empty flattery, he mentions only his dignity. And what does Christ say? Putting down the Devil's pride, and showing that in what had happened, although the Devil had not mentioned it, there was nothing shameful, nothing unworthy of his wisdom, he himself speaks openly about it and says *one does not live by bread alone.*[2] Now look at the villainy of that evil spirit, how he begins his attack, and how he forgets none of his skill. He begins weaving his trickery where he had begun when he cast out the first man and entangled him in a thousand evils: that is, with the stomach's lack of self-control.[3] You can hear many foolish people nowadays talking about a thousand evils that arise because of the stomach, but Christ shows that a virtuous person cannot be compelled by the stomach's tyranny to do anything that is not suitable. He endures hunger, refusing to obey its commands. Thus we are taught not to obey the Devil in anything.

Since the first man came into conflict with God because of his stomach and transgressed the law, Jesus goes beyond what is strictly necessary and teaches you not to obey it even when what it commands is not sinful. Why do I mention sin? 'Even if the devils say something useful', says Jesus, 'do not listen to them'. Similarly, he commanded those devils who were proclaiming him to be the Son of God to be silent. What does he say? *One does not live by bread alone.* What he means is this: God can feed the hungry even by a single word. He calls the Old Testament to witness as he teaches us that whenever we are hungry, whenever we suffer, we must not depart from the Lord. (Saint John Chrysostom)[4]

2. Sunday Year B

The Spirit immediately drove him out into the wilderness. He was in the wilderness forty days, tempted by Satan; and he was with the wild beasts; and the angels waited on him.[5]

Matthew similarly, after telling of the baptism of the Lord and the voice from heaven saying *This is my Son, the Beloved, with whom I am well pleased,*[6] immediately continued *Then Jesus was led into the wilderness by the Spirit, that he might be tempted by the Devil.*[7] But, lest a doubt arise as to what Spirit they meant, by whom he was led or driven into the desert, Luke deliberately said first that *Jesus, full of the Holy Spirit, returned from the Jordan,* and then added *and was led by the Spirit into the wilderness,*[8] so that nobody should think that an unclean spirit had power over him who, full of the Holy Spirit, went where he wished and did what he wished.

The forty days and nights during which he tempts him stand for the whole history of this world, during which he never ceases to tempt his members, that is, Holy Church. This is because the world in which we serve the Lord is divided into four parts, and there are ten commandments, by observing which as servants of the Lord we fight against the wickedness of our tireless enemy. Ten times four makes forty, and so the total duration of our warfare is aptly signified by forty days and forty nights.

So the Lord after his baptism is driven out by the Spirit into the wilderness and tempted by Satan, to give his faithful an example of how to live: after they have received the forgiveness of sins in baptism, they must be ready not only to do virtuous deeds, but also to endure persecution for the sake of justice. He retires to the desert in order to teach us to leave the enticements of the world and the company of the wicked, and to obey God's commandments in all things. He is tempted in solitude by the Devil to teach us that all who wish to live holy lives in Christ suffer persecution, and that *it is through many persecutions that we must enter the kingdom of God*.[9] He is tempted for forty days and forty nights to teach us that for as long as we live here in the Lord's service, whether we enjoy good times (of which the days are a sign) or endure adversity (symbolised by the nights), the enemy is always there, throughout the world, threatening those who walk in the law of the Lord, never ceasing to block our way with his temptations.

And he was with the wild beasts; and the angels waited on him.[10] He lives among the beasts as man, but he enjoys the ministry of the angels as God. And when in the desert of a holy life we suffer with pure minds the bestial ways of men, we are rewarded with the ministry of angels, by whom, when we are free of our bodies, we are carried to the eternal joys of heaven. (Saint Bede)[11]

3. Sunday Year C

Then Jesus was led into the desert by the Spirit, that he might be tempted by the devil.[12]

It is good to remember how the first Adam was cast out of paradise into the desert, so that you may realise how the second Adam returned from the desert to paradise. See how the bondage of old judgments is undone and how God's generosity renews itself. Adam was made from the virgin soil,

Christ is from a Virgin; Adam was made according to the image of God, Christ is the image of God; Adam was set above all irrational animals, Christ above all living things; through a woman came folly, through the Virgin wisdom; through the tree death, through the Cross life. Adam, being naked of spiritual adornments, clothed himself in leaves stripped from a tree; Christ, being naked of all worldliness, had no desire for bodily clothing. Adam was in the desert, Christ is in the desert: for he knew where to find the one who was lost, so as to call him back to paradise, freeing him from the error of his wandering ways. But since he could not return while dressed in worldly clothing, nor can anybody become a dweller in paradise who is not naked of blame, he removes the old man and puts on the new. Thus, since divine judgments cannot be reversed, it is the person judged rather than the judgment that is changed.

But how can one who, without anybody to lead him, lost the way that had been shown him in paradise, find again in the desert, without a guide, the way that he has lost? There are many temptations in the desert: the struggle for virtue is difficult, it is easy to fall into error. Virtue is like a tree. If in its youth, while it is still weak and tender, it grows up from the earth high into the sky, although thickly covered with foliage, it is vulnerable to the gnawings of cruel disease and is easily cut down or burnt up. But a robust tree with deep roots and strong branches is attacked in vain by the teeth of wild beasts, the hands of countryfolk or the blowing of winds from all directions.

Whom then could he send as guide against so many worldly allurements, so many tricks of the Devil, knowing as he did that the fight is first against *blood and flesh*, then *against the rulers, against the authorities, against the cosmic powers of this present darkness, against the spiritual forces of evil in the heavenly places?*[13] Should he send an angel? Angels too have fallen. Legions of them have hardly been enough to save individuals.[14] Should he send the Seraphim? A seraph

23

descended to earth among a people of unclean lips and cleansed the lips of only one prophet by placing coal on them. There was need for another guide, whom all might follow. Who could be so great a guide as to bring benefit to all, if not he who is above all? Who can set me above the world except he who is greater than the world? Who could be so great a guide as to be able to lead together male and female, *Greek and Jew, barbarian, Scythian, slave and free, except Christ, who is all and in all?*[15] (Saint Ambrose)[16]

4. Monday

Then the king will say to those at his right hand, Come, you that are blessed by my Father, inherit the kingdom prepared for you from the foundation of the world; for I was hungry and you gave me food, I was thirsty and you gave me something to drink, I was a stranger and you welcomed me, I was naked and you gave me clothing, I was sick and you took care of me, I was in prison and you visited me.... Truly I tell you, just as you did it to one of the least of these who are members of my family, you did it to me.[17]

See how easy his commandments are. He does not say 'I was in prison and you set me free, I was sick and you raised me up', but *you visited me* and *you came to me*. Nor in the case of hunger is his command oppressive. He did not seek an expensive meal, but only what is necessary, the food he needed, and he sought it in the clothes of a beggar, so that they deserved punishment on account of everything: the easiness of the request, since it was for bread; the pitiable character of the one asking, since he was poor; his appeal to natural sympathy, since he was a man; the desirableness of the promise, since he promised a kingdom; the fearful nature of the punishment, since he threatened hell; the worthiness of the one receiving, since it was God receiving through the poor; the great honour he was bestowing, in that he stooped so low; the justice of his request, since what he was asking for was his own. But those who were enslaved by covetousness were unable to respond to all these things, even in face of so great a threat. Earlier he had said that those who do not receive such people will suffer worse than Sodom.[18] And then he says *just as you did not do it to one of the least of these, you did not do it to me.*[19] What do you say, Lord? They are your brethren: and how do you call them least? They are your brethren because they are humble, because they are poor, because they are outcasts. These are they whom he most calls into brotherhood, the unknown, those whom it is easy to look down on. By these he not only means monks and people who have gone to live in the mountains, but each and every believer. Although a person may be living a life in the world, if he is hungry and suffering from malnutrition, and naked, and a foreigner, Jesus wills that he should receive all these acts of kindness, for every person who is baptized and partakes in the divine mysteries becomes a member of the brotherhood. (Saint John Chrysostom)[20]

5. Tuesday

Pray then in this way: Our Father in heaven.[21]

See how he immediately stirred up his hearer, reminding him at once of all God's goodness. He who calls God Father acknowledges with that one title the taking away of sins, the removal of punishment, justice, holiness, redemption, adoption, inheritance, brotherhood with the only-begotten Son, and the gift of the Spirit, since it is not possible to call God Father without having received all these blessings. So he raises their spirits in two ways, by the worthiness of him who is called on, and by the greatness of the blessings which they have enjoyed. But when he says *in heaven* he does not say it as if he were shutting God up there, but in order to lead the person praying away from the earth, establishing him in the high places and in the dwellings that are above.

He teaches us to make a common prayer, on behalf of our brothers and sisters. He does not say 'My Father, who art in heaven', but OUR FATHER, raising up prayers for the common body, and nowhere caring for his own concerns, but everywhere for the concerns of his neighbour. And by this he takes away enmity, throws down pride, casts out malice and brings in charity, the mother of all good things. He banishes inequality from human affairs, and reveals a great equality between the king and the poor man, for in those things that are greatest and most necessary we are all sharers. What harm comes of our being brothers and sisters below since we are all companions in what is above, nobody having more than another, neither the rich man more than the poor man, nor the master more than the slave, nor the ruler more than the subject, nor the king more than the soldier, nor the philosopher more than the barbarian, nor the wise man more than the idiot? He has conferred nobility on everybody by allowing all alike to call him *Father*. (Saint John Chrysostom)[22]

6. Wednesday

> *This generation is an evil generation; it asks for a sign, but no sign will be given to it except the sign of Jonah. For just as Jonah became a sign to the people of Nineveh, so the Son of Man will be to this generation.*[23]

Here is expressed the mystery of the Church, which is gathered from the ends of the whole earth, with the Ninevites because of their penitence,[24] and with the Queen of the South because of her care to discover wisdom.[25] The Church is gathered in order to hear the words of Solomon the peacemaker. She is evidently a queen, whose kingdom is undivided, rising up from the distant peoples to become one body. And so this is a great mystery, and I am applying it to Christ and the Church,[26] but this is yet greater, for that went before as a prefiguration, but now the mystery is fulfilled in truth: there was Solomon, the foreshadowing, but here is Christ in his body. So the life of the Church depends on these two things, either that you do not know how to sin, or that you cease to sin: for penitence abolishes sin, and wisdom takes precautions against it.

The sign of Jonah, which is a foreshadowing of the Lord's passion, also witnesses to the grave sins of those who put him to death. So Jesus' words are both a prophecy, issuing from his divine majesty, and a sign of his mercy. He speaks both of the punishment with which the people of Nineveh were threatened and of the remedy against sin, that is repentance, which was offered to them. So those who sin against Christ have no need to despair of his pardon, if they are willing to do penance. (Saint Ambrose)[27]

7. Thursday

Ask, and it will be given you; search, and you will find; knock, and the door will be opened for you.[28]

The Lord says not only that his disciples must exert themselves, but also that they must call down help from above: and he will certainly come and be with us and stand by us in our trials and make everything easy for us. That was why he told us to ask and promised that what we ask would be given us. Moreover, he did not tell us simply to *ask*, but to do so persistently and eagerly, for that is what *search* means. A searcher puts everything else out of his mind and is concerned only with what he is searching for, quite unaware of those around him. Anybody who is looking for gold or a servant he has lost understands what I am saying. That is what Jesus means by *search*. As for *knock*, by that he means that we should approach God earnestly and with an ardent

27

spirit. Do not allow yourself to slide, do not show less enthusiasm about virtue than you do about possessions. Often you have searched for things and not found them and yet, even when you knew you were not going to find them, you did everything you possibly could to search them out. In this case, you have already heard good news about things you are certainly going to receive, and yet you do not show about them even the tiniest part of the enthusiasm you show over material possessions. If you do not receive straight away, do not let that make you give up hope. That was why he said *knock*, to indicate that even if he does not open the door at once, you must stay there. <> Think about this, and do not give up until you *receive*, do not go away until you *find*, do not stop knocking until the door is *opened*. If you keep this thought in mind, and say 'unless I receive, I will not go away' you certainly will receive, provided you ask for things that he can rightly give, things that will be good for you. What sort of things are they? That you may seek all the spiritual gifts; that you may behave towards those who ask forgiveness as one who has himself been forgiven; that you may lift up *holy hands without anger or argument*.[29] If that is how we ask, we shall receive. At present our asking is a joke, more like that of drunkards than of sober people. 'What if I do not receive even when I ask for spiritual things?' I hear you say. You did not knock earnestly, or you made yourself unworthy to receive, or you went away too quickly. 'Why then', you ask 'did he not tell us what we should ask?' He has told you already, and shown you what things you should approach God for. So do not say 'I went to him and did not receive'. That is not the fault of God, whose love is stronger than that of our fathers, as much stronger as good is stronger than evil. *If you then, who are evil, know how to give good gifts to your children, how much more will your Father in heaven give good things to those who ask him!*[30] He said this, not to find fault with our nature or to speak ill of the human race, but to tell us that a father's love, compared with the goodness of God, is no better than malice. So great is God's love for us. (Saint John Chrysostom)[31]

8. Friday

So when you are offering your gift at the altar, if you remember that your brother or sister has something against you, leave your gift there before the altar and go; first be reconciled to your brother or sister, and then come and offer your gift.[32]

See the utter goodness and kindness of the Lord! His own honour is less important to him than the love of our neighbour. <> Could words be more gentle than these? 'Let my worship be interrupted that your love may remain.' He did not say 'after you have offered' or 'before you offer', but while the gift is lying there, when the sacrifice has already begun, for reconciliation is itself a sacrifice. We are not to pick up our gift again, or to be reconciled before we put it down, but while it is lying there in front of everybody he tells us to run and find our brother. Why? For two reasons, I think. Firstly, as he himself said, because he holds love in great honour, considering it the greatest of sacrifices, without which he does not accept the gifts we bring to the altar. Secondly, to lay on us an obligation to be reconciled against which there is no excuse. Somebody who has been told not to offer a gift before being reconciled will be impelled to run to the one he has hurt and put an end to the enmity between them, if not out of love for his neighbour, then at least because he does not want to leave his gift lying there with the ceremony unfinished. That is why the Lord spoke so emphatically, to strike fear into such a person and arouse him. He said *leave your gift there*, but he did not stop at that: he added *before the altar* (a place the very mention of which is enough to make one tremble) *and go*. To *go* he added *first* and *then come and offer your gift*: all this was to teach us that this table does not receive those who are at enmity with one another. <> So if you pray with enmity in your heart, it would be better to stop praying and go to be reconciled to your brother or sister, and then offer your prayer. <> That was why God became human and did all that he did, to bring us together. <> 'For if you are reconciled', he says, 'because of your love towards your brother or sister, you will find me merciful towards you as well, and you can bring your sacrifice to the altar in all confidence. But if you are still smouldering, remember that I am gladly telling you to forget what belongs to me, so that you may be friends again.' Let that thought calm your anger. Even if the resentment is just, that does not mean that you should continue it, for Christ was justly angry with us, but nonetheless he gave himself to death for us, not counting our sins against us. (Saint John Chrysostom)[33]

9. Saturday

I say to you, Love your enemies and pray for those who persecute you.[34]

Jesus did not only tell us to love our enemies, but to pray for them. Do you see the steps up which he has walked to bring us to this highest point of virtue? Consider them, and count them from the beginning.[35] The first step is not to cause injustice; the second is, where injustice has begun, not to defend oneself against it by injustice in return; the third, not to repay one who harms us with similar harm, but to remain quiet; the fourth, to offer ourselves for ill-treatment; the fifth, to offer more than our enemy desires; the sixth, not to hate a person who has done such things; the seventh, to love that person; the eighth, to do good to him; the ninth, to pray to God for him. Do you see that this is the summit of wisdom? That is why it receives a splendid reward. Because it is a great commandment, demanding vigour of soul and serious commitment, the Lord rewards it like none of the preceding ones. He does not here offer the earth, as he did to the meek, or mercy and comfort as to the merciful and those who mourn, or even the kingdom of heaven. No, he offers something more awe-inspiring than all of those: to become like God, in so far as that is possible for humans. He says *so that you may be children of your Father in heaven*.[36] <> Do not hate a person who ill-treats you, since he gives you such great gifts and is leading you to such high honour; do not curse anyone who abuses you, for you will still undergo pain, and yet be deprived of its fruit: you will suffer loss, and not receive your payment. It is the ultimate madness to endure greater pains and not to bear lesser ones. How can this be? When you see God become human, so great a being having descended so low and having suffered such terrible things for you, you are still puzzled and ask how it is possible for us to forgive our fellow-servants the injustices they commit. Do you not hear him saying to you from the Cross, *Forgive them for they do not know what they are doing*?[37] Do you not hear Paul saying, *It is Christ Jesus, who died, yes, who was raised, who is at the right hand of God, who indeed intercedes for us*?[38] Do you not see how, after his cross and resurrection, he sent his apostles with a thousand good gifts to those who had killed him, who might have expected to suffer from him a thousand torments? Have you suffered great injustice? Have you suffered as much as your Lord, bound, scourged, slapped in the face, spat on by slaves, made to suffer the most shameful death of all, after the myriad good deeds he had done? Even if you have suffered great injustice, that is a reason for doing great good, that your crown may be brighter and your brother released from mortal sickness. (Saint John Chrysostom)[39]

NOTES

1. Matt 4:3
2. Matt 4:4
3. cf. Gen 3:1
4. *Commentary on Matthew* 13, 2; *PG* 57, 210-211
5. Mark 1:12
6. Matt 3:17
7. Matt 4:1
8. Luke 4:1
9. Acts 14:22
10. Mark 1:13
11. *Commentary on Mark* 1,1; *PL* 92, 139-140
12. Matt 4:1; cf. Luke 4:1-2
13. Eph 6:12
14. cf. 2 Kings 6:17
15. cf. Col 3:11
16. *Commentary on Luke* 4, 7-9; *PL* 15, 1697-1698
17. Matt 25:34-36;40
18. Matt 10:15
19. Matt 25:45
20. *Commentary on Matthew* 79, 1; *PG* 58, 718
21. Matt 6:9
22. *Commentary on Matthew* 19,4; *PG* 57, 278-279
23. Luke 11:29
24. cf. Jonah 3:5
25. cf. 1 Kings 10
26. Eph 5:32
27. *Commentary on Luke* 7, 96-97; *PL* 15, 1812
28. Matt 7:7
29. 1 Tim 2:8
30. Matt 7:11
31. *Commentary on Matthew* 23, 4; *PG* 57, 312-313
32. Matt 5:23-24
33. *Commentary on Matthew* 16, 9; *PG* 57, 250-251
34. Matt 5:44

35. cf. Matt 5:21-48
36. Matt 5:45
37. Luke 23:34
38. Rom 8:34
39. *Commentary on Matthew* 18, 4; *PG* 57, 269-270

3

THE SECOND WEEK OF LENT

1. Sunday Year A

Six days later, Jesus took with him Peter and James and his brother John and led them up a high mountain, by themselves. And he was transfigured before them, his face shone like the sun, and his clothes became dazzling white.[1]

What does the hot-headed Peter say? *It is good for us to be here.*[2] He has heard that Jesus must go to Jerusalem and suffer, and he is troubled and fearful about him even after Jesus has rebuked him, he dare not come to him again and say *God forbid it!*,[3] but he hints again at the same thing in different words because of his fear. For when he saw the mountain, and how remote and deserted it was, he realised that Jesus would be very safe there, not only because of the nature of the terrain, but also because if Jesus remained there he would no longer go to Jerusalem. He wanted him to stay there for ever, which is why he mentioned dwellings. 'If this happens', he means, 'we shall not go up to Jerusalem; if we do not go up, he will not die, since that is where he said the scribes would lay hands on him'. <>

Although Peter said *I will make three dwellings*,[4] Jesus showed him a *house not made with hands*[5] <> with indescribable light and a voice. <> And what does the voice say? *This is my Son, the Beloved.*[6] If he is beloved, Peter, then do not be afraid. You should already be aware of his power, and full of confidence in the Resurrection, but since you are still uncertain, take courage from the voice of the Father. If God is mighty, as he certainly is, then it is plain that the Son is mighty as well. So do not be afraid of any danger. And if you still do not understand, consider that he is both a Son and the

Beloved. <> Since he is beloved, have no fear, for nobody gives up the one he loves. Do not be troubled. However much you love him, you do not love him as much as the Father who begot him. <> He loves him not only because he is his Father, but also because he is in every way equal to him and of the same mind. So this love is twofold, or rather three-fold, since he is a Son, he is Beloved, he is pleasing. What does *With him I am well pleased*[7] mean? It is as if he had said 'I find my rest and my delight in him', since he is perfectly equal with him in every way; there is one will in him and in the Father, and he is one with the Father in all respects, although he remains a Son. *Listen to him!*:[8] even if he wills to be crucified, you must not oppose him.

So there is nothing more blessed than the Apostles, and especially those three who were found worthy to be under the Lord's roof,[9] even in the cloud. But we also, if he will, shall see Christ, not as they saw him then on the mountain, but shining with far greater brightness. For when he comes again he will not be as he was then. Then, to spare the disciples, he showed them a glimpse of as much of his brightness as they were able to bear, but he will come again in the very glory of the Father, not only with Moses and Elijah, but with the innumerable army of the angels, with the archangels, with the Cherubim, with that whole company which cannot be counted. There will be no cloud around his head, but the entire heavens will be humbled beneath his feet. (Saint John Chrysostom)[10]

2. Sunday Year B

And his clothing became shining, as white as snow.[11]

In his transfiguration the Saviour did not lose the real sub-stance of his human flesh, but showed the glory of the com-ing resurrection, both his and ours, for as he appeared then to the apostles he will appear after the judgment to all the chosen. On the day of judgment he will appear both to the good and the bad in the form of a servant, so that the wicked may look on him whom they spurned, the Jews on him whom they denied, the soldiers on him whom they crucified, Pilate and Herod on him whom they condemned, and recognise him as their judge. The Lord's clothing is rightly understood to be holy, for the Apostle Paul says *as many of you as were baptized into Christ have clothed yourselves with Christ.*[12] When the Lord was on earth his clothes were humble and seemed like the clothes of others, but when he went up the mountain they shone with a new brightness, for *we are God's children now, but what we will be has not yet been revealed. What we do know is this: when he is revealed, we will be like him, for we will see him as he is.*[13]

It is appropriate that these clothes are said to be *whiter,*[14] for Jesus here is to be understood to be the fuller to whom the psalmist prays in penitence *wash me,*[15] and he cannot give to his faithful on earth the glory that is stored up for them in heaven.[16] *And there appeared to them Elijah with Moses, who were talking with Jesus.*[17] Moses and Elijah, of whom we read that one died[18] and the other was taken up into heaven,[19] and who were *seen in glory*[20] with the Lord, as Luke says, are a sign of the glory that all the saints will have in him. Whether they are found alive in the flesh on the Day of Judgment or have already tasted death, they will be raised up and reign with him, as the apostle says: *The dead in Christ will rise first. Then we who are alive, who are left, will be caught up in the clouds together with them to meet the Lord in the air; and so we will be with the Lord forever.*[21] <>

Finally, the children of Israel were able to see Moses, but were not allowed to follow him when he went up the mountain to God, nor could they look at him when he came back to them unless he wore a veil.[22] They did know Elijah, but only Elisha with the sons of the prophets contemplated his triumph as he ascended into heaven,[23] for there are many of us who read the words of Holy Scripture, but very few people, the more perfect among us, understand its depth and splendour, filled as it is with the mysteries of Christ. (Saint Bede)[24]

3. Sunday Year C

Jesus took with him Peter and John and James, and went up on the mountain to pray.[25]

Let us rise above worldly activity that we may see God face to face. I might understand the number three to stand for the whole human race, since we are all descended from the three sons of Noah.[26] Alternatively, it may refer to the chosen ones of God, since only those who confess Christ will be found worthy to share in the grace of the resurrection. <> So three are chosen to go up the mountain, because two are chosen to be seen with the Lord. Both these are sacred numbers. Three is perhaps sacred because nobody can see the glory of the resurrection who has not kept the mystery of the Trinity with pure and incorrupt faith. Peter went up, who received the keys of the kingdom of heaven, John, to whom the Lord's Mother was entrusted, and James, the first of the disciples to occupy a bishop's throne. Then Moses and Elijah appear, that is, the Law and the Prophet together with the Word, for the Law cannot exist without the Word, nor is there any prophet who has not prophesied concerning the Son of God. Those sons of thunder looked on Moses and Elijah in bodily glory, but we too look every day on Moses with the Son of God, for we see the Law in the Gospel when we read *You shall love the Lord your God,*[27] and we see Elijah with the Word of God when we read *Behold, a virgin shall conceive.*[28]

These things are mysteries which call us to climb higher. According to your capacity the Word grows greater or lesser for you: unless you climb the peak of higher knowledge, wisdom is not revealed to you, nor the understanding of mysteries. You do not see how great glory and beauty there is in

God's Word, but the Word appears as if clothed in a body, without his form and majesty, like a wounded man, who is able to sympathise with our weaknesses: he seems to be like a human word, wrapped in dark obscurity, not radiant with the power of the Spirit. But if, when you consider the man Jesus, you believe that he was born of a virgin, and faith gradually inspires you to believe that he was born of the Spirit of God, then you begin to go up the mountain. If you see him on the cross, not destroyed but triumphing over death, if you see that the earth trembled, the sun fled, the eyes of unbelievers were covered in darkness, tombs were opened, the dead rose – as a sign that the gentile peoples, who were dead to God, rose as if their tombs had been opened when the light of the cross shone on them – if you see this mystery, then you have gone up the highest mountain and you are gazing on the Word in the second manifestation of his glory. (Saint Ambrose)[29]

4. Monday

Be merciful, just as your Father is merciful.[30]

God's generosity extends far and wide: he sheds his rain on the ungrateful, so that the fruitful earth lavishes its bounty even on the wicked. The same sun shines on religious and irreligious people alike. If we interpret this verse in a mystical sense, we can say that the teachings of the prophets were the rains with which God irrigated the people of Israel, and that he shone on them with the rays of the eternal sun, even though they were unworthy. But because they were steeped in the dew of worldliness, the church of God has been brought into his heavenly light, while his promises still hold good for the Jewish people, if they trust in his mercy. <>

A good measure, gathered together, running over, will be given to you.[31] What can I say about water? The Holy Spirit hovered over the water before the very birth of the world, as you can read in the Scriptures. O Water, mixed with human blood, you washed the whole earth in a prefiguring of the washing of baptism that we know today. You were counted worthy to be a sacramental sign of Christ, for you wash all things but are yourself not washed. You are at the beginning and at the completion of God's mysteries. In you is the beginning, in you the end, or rather, it is because of you that we know no end. By you the filth of decaying flesh is done away with and our decaying corpses, sprinkled with salt, are preserved for all ages. From you our bodies, exhausted by heat, receive a drink delicious with grace, healthy for life, sweet and delightful; you have given a name to prophets and apostles, and to our saviour himself, for the prophets are the clouds of the heavens,[32] the apostles the salt of the earth,[33] and he himself is the fountain of life.[34] Confined among the mountains, you are not impeded in your course, dashed upon rocks you remain unshattered, poured out over the earth you are not expended, but gushing in tiny streams you infuse the spirit of life into the plants you fill, you give fertile moisture to those around which you flow, your streams give assistance to those over which you are showered, lest the earth, exhausted because her vital parts are dry, should neglect to bring forth her yearly plenty. You are found in all four quarters of the universe, in the sky, the air, the sea and the earth. When the prophet Moses struck the rock it poured you forth to refresh the dry hearts of the people;[35] when you flowed from the side of the saviour,[36] those who struck him saw and believed, and so you are one of the three witnesses of our regeneration, for there are *three that testify, the Spirit, and the water, and the blood*,[37] the water of our cleansing, the blood the price of our redemption, the Spirit who raises us to life. (Saint Ambrose)[38]

5. Tuesday

Then Jesus said to the crowds and to his disciples, 'The scribes and the Pharisees sit on Moses' seat; therefore, do

> *whatever they teach you and follow it; but do not do as they*
> *do, for they do not practise what they teach.'*[39]

To set them on the right path, he commands above all that which comes first among the things that lead to salvation, namely not to hold one's teachers in contempt, nor to rise up against the priests. And not only does he command this, but he practises it himself. Although they are corrupt, he does not deprive them of their honour, which makes their crime the greater, and leaves his disciples no excuse for disobedience. Nobody can say 'my teacher was evil, so I grew slack', since he has taken away this excuse. Such was the honour he gave them, although they were evil, that after accusing them so fiercely he said *do whatever they teach you and follow it*, for the laws they teach are not their own but God's, given through Moses. See what respect he shows to Moses, again demonstrating the harmony of his own teaching with the old Law and honouring its teachers when he says they *sit on Moses' seat*. He could not honour them because of their way of life, so he honours them as he can, because of their seat and their succession from Moses. When you hear him say *whatever*, do not think that that means everything in the Law, such as the precepts about food, sacrifices and suchlike. How could he mean that, when he had already done away with such precepts? By *whatever* he means things that correct our way of life and make it better, things that agree with the commandments of the new law and no longer allow us to be under the yoke of the law. <> Why does he criticise them, and speak at such length on this subject? To warn the people against falling into the same sins. <> Consider how he begins his accusation and then intensifies it: *they teach you*, he says, and *they do not practise what they teach*. Everybody who transgresses the law is worthy of condemnation, but especially one who has authority to teach: such a one deserves a double and a triple condemnation, firstly because of his transgression, secondly because his duty is to correct others and yet he does it falteringly, and so deserves greater punishment because of his position, and thirdly because he has greater power to corrupt by virtue of his teaching office. After all this the Lord adds another reason for condemnation, that they are cruel to those over whom they are set: *They tie up heavy burdens, hard to bear, and lay them on the shoulders of others; but they themselves are unwilling to lift a finger to move them.*[40] He is speaking here of a double wickedness: without mercy they require great and lofty purity of life from their subjects, while allowing themselves considerable freedom. This is exactly the opposite of what a good superior should do, which is to be a cruel and merciless judge in everything that concerns himself but gentle and forgiving in what concerns his subjects. (Saint John Chrysostom)[41]

6. Wednesday

'You know that the rulers of the Gentiles lord it over them, and their great ones are tyrants over them. It will not be so among you; but whoever wishes to be great among you must be your servant, and whoever wishes to be first among you must be your slave; just as the Son of Man came not to be served but to serve, and to give his life a ransom for many.'[42]

Let us think this out rationally. A person is said to be 'high' who is tall in body or who stands on a high place, and a person is 'low' who is or does the opposite. Now, let us consider whether a boastful person or a modest one is 'high': this will help you to see that nothing is higher than humility or lower than pride. A boaster wants to be greater than everybody else and claims that nobody is worthy of him, and however much honour he achieves he always claims and longs for more and thinks he has nothing; he despises other human beings and longs for the honour that they have. Could anything be more absurd? It is like a riddle: he seeks to be held in honour by the very people whom he despises. Do you see how such a person, while wanting to be exalted, falls down and lies sprawling on the ground? He shows that he considers all human beings as nothing compared with himself, such is his arrogance. Why would one rush towards a person who is nobody? Why seek honour from him? Why bother with these crowds of nobodies? You see, he is 'low', for he is standing on those who are low.

Now let us consider who is 'high'. He knows what it is to be human, that a human being is a great thing, and that he is the last of all, and so he values highly whatever honour comes his way. His life makes sense, he is 'high' and his thinking is coherent: he considers great the honours he receives from those whom he considers great, even when they are small, because the source from which they come is great. But the boastful man thinks that those who honour him are nothing, while the honours they give are great. The humble man is not conquered by any suffering, no passion will be able to trouble him, or the love of glory, malice or jealousy. What could be higher than a soul freed from these things? But a proud person is in the grip of all of them like a worm writhing in the mud, for jealousy and malice and anger are always troubling his soul. Now who is 'high', a person who is above sufferings, or one who is their slave? One who lives in fear of them, or one who is unconquered and never overcome by them? Which bird would we say was higher, the one that is above the hands and traps of the hunter, or one that the hunter does not even need a trap to catch, since it flies along the ground and can never soar towards the sky? That is what a proud man is like: any trap can easily catch him as he crawls along the ground. (Saint John Chrysostom)[43]

7. Thursday

There was a rich man who dressed in purple.[44]

This seems to be more a story than a parable, since even the

42

name of this man is given.[45] But there is in fact a deeper meaning to what the Lord says about this rich man who, when his worldly pleasures were over, was in perpetual hunger in hell and who, significantly, is said to have five brothers. They stand for our five bodily senses[46] which are related like five brothers, inflamed with innumerable immoderate desires, whereas the Lord placed Lazarus with Abraham as if in a haven of rest and a hiding-place of holiness, to teach us not to remain in our vices, ensnared by the desires of this present world, nor to avoid hardship because we are exhausted by our labours. We may think of a Lazarus, poor in the world but rich as regards God, or of some preacher of the gospel whose words may be poor but who is rich in faith, for not all poverty is holy, nor are all riches wicked, but it is luxurious living that makes riches bad, and holiness that makes poverty good. A preacher who holds the true faith does not need elaborate rhetoric <> but, if he restrains the desires of the flesh which are signified by these five brothers, he receives a rich reward, a full measure of great plenty which bears interest for ever.

We may also understand this story to be a parable about faith, which Lazarus gathered after it had been rejected from the rich man's table. The rich man would be horrified in his fastidiousness at Lazarus' rotting sores and could not bear the dogs licking them among his sumptuous banquets and finely-clad guests: the smell and the very nature of the beggar would be loathsome to him. The pride and insolence of the rich is well enough known: they are so unmindful of the human condition that they use the miseries of the poor as a source of their own pleasure, as if they were of a superior nature, and laugh at them, insult the needy, and steal from those on whom they ought to have mercy. Take whichever interpretation you like, like Lazarus beside the rich man's table. <>

Think now of the Arians[47] with their worldly ambitions, who associate themselves with the power of the Emperor so that they can use military weapons to attack the truth of the Church: do they not seem to you to be dressed in purple and fine linen and lying on banqueting-couches, so as to defend their lies as if they were true? They make impressive speeches about how the earth trembled when the Lord walked over it, the sky was covered in darkness, the sea was roused into tempest and then stilled, and yet they deny that he was the Son of God. Think of the poor man, who knows that the kingdom of God is not a matter of talk but of virtue and professes his faith in a few words when he says *You are... the Son of the living God.*[48] Do not their riches seem to you to be poor, and his poverty to be rich? Wealthy heretics have written any number of gospels, but the poor faithful hold only the one gospel they have received; rich philosophers have made themselves many gods, while the Church in her poverty knows only the one God. (Saint Ambrose)[49]

8. Friday

> *'Listen to another parable. There was a landowner who planted a vineyard, put a fence around it, dug a wine press in it, and built a watchtower. Then he leased it to tenants and went to another country. When the harvest time had come, he sent his slaves to the tenants to collect his produce. But the tenants seized his slaves and beat one, killed another, and stoned another. Again he sent other slaves, more than the first; and they treated them in the same way. Finally he sent his son to them, saying, "They will respect my son." But when the tenants saw the son, they said to themselves, "This is the heir; come, let us kill him and get his inheritance." So they seized him, threw him out of the vineyard, and killed him.'*[50]

The Lord is suggesting several things to his hearers in this parable: God's providence, which has always been with his people; their murderous spirit from the beginning; the fact that he has left undone nothing that could help them, and that even after the slaughter of the prophets he did not turn away from them but even sent his Son; that there is one God of both the Old and the New Testaments; the great and beneficial effects of his death, that they will suffer the Last Judgment on their crimes, and his crucifixion, the call of the gentiles and the falling-away of the Jews. <> Consider now God's great care for them, and their indescribable laziness. He himself did the work of the farmer, digging a ditch, planting the vineyard, and everything else, leaving them a small task, to take care of those things and guard what he had given them. Nothing had been forgotten: everything was as it should be. Yet they did not profit even by the great gifts he had given them. For when they came out of Egypt, he gave them the law, and founded a city for them and built them a Temple. *And he went to another country*, that is, he was very patient, not always punishing them immediately for their sins. <> He sent his slaves, that is, the prophets, *to collect his produce*, that is, their obedience, shown in their works. Then they showed their wickedness, not by having no produce to give after all the care they had received, for that was mere laziness, but by receiving badly those who came to them. It would have been suitable for people who owed something they could not pay not to grow angry or resentful, but to ask for help. They did not only show anger, but filled their hands with blood, and made demands when it was they in fact who were the debtors. So the landowner sent messengers a second and a third time, so that the tenants' wickedness and his own kindness might be clearly seen. <> Even if they were arrogant towards the servants, they ought to have respected the dignity of the son. And what did they do? They ought to have run up to him and asked forgiveness for their sins, but instead they strove to outdo themselves in wrongdoing, setting themselves to do further evil and piling new sins on top of their former ones. <> But they did not come to their senses, even though they had received the commandment *you shall not murder*[51] and been commanded to abstain from so many things because of this, and had so many and various reasons for keeping that commandment. Still they did not put away their wicked habit. What did they say when they saw him? *Come, let us kill him.*

Why did you say that? What crime, small or large, did you have to accuse him of? That he honoured you, although he was God, and became human for you, and performed so many wonderful deeds? Because he forgave sins? Because he called you to the Kingdom? (Saint John Chrysostom)[52]

9. Saturday

> *There was a man who had two sons. The younger of them said to his father, 'Father, give me the share of the property that will belong to me'.*[53]

Do not blame the father for giving the property to the younger brother, for you know that God's inheritance is given to all who ask. In the kingdom of God there is no such thing as 'tender years', nor does faith grow old with our advancing years.

Certainly the son who asked for his inheritance thought it right that he should receive it. If only he had not left his father, he would not have learnt that his youth was a handicap. But after he *travelled to a distant country* and left his father's house, *he began to be in need.*[54] Similarly, anybody who leaves the Church is squandering his inheritance. <> To leave one's self is to make a far longer journey than anybody who travels to another country. But to be separated in one's way of life, to be different in one's values rather than one's country, to suffer divorce, as it were, in one's way of life because the passion for worldly luxury has cut one off – what of that? Whoever separates himself from Christ is an exile from his fatherland and a citizen of this world. But we are not *strangers and aliens,* but we are *citizens with the saints and also members of the household of God;*[55] we *who once were far off have been brought near by the blood of Christ.*[56] Let us not be envious of people who come back from long journeys, for we too have been in a far country, as Isaiah says: *The people who walked in the land of the shadow of death have seen a great light.*[57] The land of the shadow of death is a long way away, but we, whose very breath of life[58] is Christ the Lord, live in the shadow of Christ. That is why the Church says *with great delight I sat in his shadow.*[59] The prodigal son by his luxurious way of life ruined everything that nature had given him. You, who have been made in the likeness of God and have received his image,[60] do not allow it to be ruined by the filth of irrational desires.

He would gladly have filled himself with the pods.[61] Those who live self-indulgently have no care other than to fill themselves: *their god is the belly.*[62] What food could be more suitable for people like that than pods which are soft outside but empty within, which fill the body without nourishing it, and give more bulk than nourishment? <>

Lord Jesus, take away our pods and give us bread, for you are the steward in the Father's house; make us your hired servants and lead us to your vineyard, although we come late! You bring some to your vineyard at the eleventh hour and pay them a wage equal to the others,[63] an equal wage of life, not of glory, for not to all *there is reserved the crown of righteousness,*[64] but to those who can say *I have fought the good fight.*[65] (Saint Ambrose)[66]

NOTES

1. Matt 17:1-2
2. Matt 17:4
3. Matt 16:22
4. Matt 17:4
5. cf. Mark 14:58; 2 Cor 5:1; Heb 9:11, 24

6. Matt 17:5
7. Matt 17:5
8. Matt 17:5
9. cf. Matt 8:8
10. *Commentary on Matthew* 56, 2-4; *PG* 58, 552-554
11. cf. Mark 9:3
12. Gal 3:27
13. 1 John 3:2
14. Mark 9:3
15. Psa 51:7
16. cf. 1 Pet 1:4
17. Mark 9:4
18. Deut 34:5
19. 2 Kings 2:11
20. Luke 9:31
21. 1 Th 4:16-17
22. Ex 34:2-3,33-35
23. 2 Kings 2:7-12
24. *Commentary on Mark* 3, 8; *PL* 92, 217-218
25. Luke 9:28
26. Gen 9:18-19
27. Matt 22:37; cf. Deut 6:5
28. Matt 1:23; cf. Is 7:14
29. *Commentary on Luke* 7, 8-12; *PL* 15, 1788-1790
30. Luke 6:36
31. Luke 6:38: modern versions translate '... will be given into your lap', but Ambrose's text of Scripture, translated here, allowed him to understand the image in this verse as being one of water.
32. Is 60:8
33. Matt 5:13
34. cf. Psa 36:9; John 7:38
35. Ex 17:6
36. John 19:34
37. 1 John 5:7
38. *Commentary on Luke* 8, 79;10, 48; *PL* 15, 1743;1907-1908

39. Matt 23:1-3
40. Matt 23:5
41. *Commentary on Matthew* 72, 1; *PG* 58, 667-668
42. Matt 20:25-28
43. *Commentary on Matthew* 65, 5; *PG* 58, 623-624
44. Luke 16:19
45. *Dives*, The Latin word for 'wealthy', was understood to be the name of the rich man in this parable: and is still widely so understood today.
46. i.e. of touch, taste, smell, hearing and sight
47. i.e. those who deny the divinity of Christ. In Ambrose's time, they included members of the Imperial family.
48. Matt 16:16
49. *Commentary on Luke* 8, 13-17; *PL* 15, 1859-1860
50. Matt 21:33-39
51. Ex 20:13
52. *Commentary on Matthew* 68, 1; *PG* 58, 639-641
53. Luke 15:11
54. Luke 15:14
55. Eph 2:19
56. Eph 2:13
57. Is 9:2
58. cf. Lam 4:20
59. Songs 2:3
60. cf. Gen 1:26
61. Luke 15:16
62. Phil 3:19
63. cf. Matt 20:1-16
64. 2 Tim 4:7-8
65. 2 Tim 4:7
66. *Commentary on Luke* 7, 213-220; *PL* 15, 1846-1848

4

THE THIRD WEEK OF LENT

1. Sunday Year A

A Samaritan woman came to draw water, and Jesus said to her, 'Give me a drink....' The Samaritan woman said to him, 'How is it that you, a Jew, ask a drink of me, a woman of Samaria?...' Jesus answered her, 'If you knew the gift of God, and who it is that is saying to you, "Give me a drink," you would have asked him, and he would have given you living water.'[1]

According to the ordinary understanding, living water is water that flows from a spring, for rain-water collected in pools and tanks is not called 'living'. If water flows from its source and then is collected somewhere which has no connection with the source, it is not called 'living': living water is water that is collected as it flows. Such was the water that was in the well where they met. So why did he promise what he was asking for?

The woman, still in suspense, says *Sir, you have no bucket, and the well is deep*[2] – you see, she thought that by *living water* he meant the water in that well. You want to give me living water, and yet it is I, not you, who am carrying a bucket to draw water. Here is living water – how are you going to give it to me? With her mistaken, material understanding she is in a way knocking at a closed door so that the master will open it. She was knocking as yet with ignorance, not with desire, as one who deserves sympathy rather than instruction.

The Lord has spoken more openly now: *The water that I will give will become in them a spring of water gushing up to eternal life. Those who drink of the water that I will give them will never be thirsty.*[3] What could be more clear than that the water he was promising was not visible, but invisible? But still the woman understood him materially: she was delighted at the thought of not being thirsty, and she thought the Lord had promised her this literally. It was her daily work to go to and fro to that well, weighed down with the burden of water that met her needs, obliged to go back again once it had been used up, and all this work quenched her thirst, but did not end it. So she was delighted at the thought of such a gift, and asked Jesus to give her living water.

Let us not pass without comment the fact that the Lord was promising something spiritual. What does he mean by *Everyone who drinks of this water will be thirsty again*?[4] This is true both of that water and of the reality of which that water was a sign. The water in the well, deep in the darkness, is worldly pleasure: people draw it up in the bucket of their desires. They allow themselves to be overcome by desire so that they may descend to the depths of pleasure and enjoy it, having first desired it. Only by beginning with desire can we arrive at pleasure. So let us say that the bucket is desire and the water from the depths is pleasure: when a person has arrived at the pleasures of this world, food, drink, the baths, public shows, sex, will he never be thirsty again? This is why Jesus says *Everyone who drinks of this water will be thirsty again*, but anybody who has water from me will never be thirsty. He says: *We shall be satisfied with the goodness of your house.*[5]

The hour is coming – when? – *and is now here* – what hour? – *when the true worshippers will worship the Father in spirit and truth*,[6] not on that mountain, nor in the temple, but *in spirit and truth*. God *is seated on high*, but he *looks far down*.[7] The Lord is near – to whom? To those who are on high? No: *to the broken-hearted*.[8] This is a wonderful thing: he lives on high, and draws near to the lowly. <> If you want to find a high and holy place, present yourself within to God as his

51

temple. *For God's temple is holy, and you are that temple.*[9] Do you wish to pray in a temple? Then pray within yourself. But first make sure that you are a temple of God, for he hears those who pray within his temple. (Saint Augustine)[10]

2. Sunday Year B

But Jesus would not entrust himself to them.[11]

What does this mean? Was it that they did not believe in him, but thought they did, and so Jesus did not entrust himself to them? Surely the evangelist would not say *many believed in his name*[12] if he were not telling the truth about them. So this is a strange and important matter: humans believe in Christ, and Christ does not entrust himself to humans. Especially because he is the Son of God, he suffered willingly: had he not been willing, he would never have suffered, just as he would not have been born had he not so willed. Had he wished to be born but not to die, he would have done that, like everything else that he willed, for he is the all-powerful Son of the all-powerful Father. <> Since Jesus had such power, which he proclaimed in his words and proved by his deeds, what does it mean that he did not entrust himself to them, as if they were going to hurt him in some way against his will or do something to him that he did not want, especially since they had already come to believe in his name? <> *Because he knew all people and needed no one to testify about anyone; for he himself knew what was in everyone.*[13] The Maker knew better what was in his work than the work knew what was in itself. The maker of humanity knew what was in humanity, while created humanity itself did not know. <>

Very truly, I tell you, no one can see the kingdom of God without being born anew:[14] this means that Jesus entrusts himself to those who are born anew. The others believed in him, and Jesus did not entrust himself to them. Such are all catechumens: they believe already in the name of Christ, but Jesus does not entrust himself to them. Listen to me in your charity and understand. If we ask a catechumen 'Do you believe in Christ?', he will answer 'I do' and sign himself with the cross. Already he carries the cross of Christ on his forehead, and is not ashamed of the sign of his Lord's cross: this means that he has believed in his name. But if we ask, 'Do you eat the flesh of the Son of Man and drink his blood?', he does not know what we are talking about, because Jesus has not entrusted himself to him.

Because catechumens bear the sign of the cross on their foreheads, they already belong to the great household of the church, but they still have to be transformed from servants into sons and daughters. Those who already belong to the great household are not nothing. But when did the people of Israel come to eat the manna? When they had crossed the Red Sea.[15] If you want to know what the Red Sea means, listen to the Apostle: *I do not want you to be unaware, brothers and sisters, that our ancestors were all under the cloud, and all passed through the sea*, and then as if you had asked him why they passed through the sea, he continues *and all were baptized into Moses in the cloud and in the sea*.[16] If the Red Sea, which was only a foreshadowing, had so powerful an effect, what will be the power of the baptism that it foreshadowed? If what happened as a figure brought the people who had crossed the sea to feast on manna, what will Christ give to his people who have passed through the waters of his true baptism? He leads believers through his baptism, killing all their sins like enemies who are pursuing them, just like all the Egyptians who perished in the Red Sea. Where does he lead them to, brethren? When Moses led his people through the sea, he was a figure of Jesus. To where does Jesus lead his people through the waters of baptism? To the manna. What is this manna? *I am the living bread*, he says, *that came down from heaven*.[17] (Saint Augustine)[18]

3. Sunday Year C

> *The Lord Jesus exhorted us to be good trees so that we may bear good fruit when he said 'Either make the tree good, and its fruit good; or make the tree bad, and its fruit bad; for the tree is known by its fruit.'* [19] <>

He is speaking against those who, although they were evil, thought they could speak good words or do good deeds. The Lord Jesus says that this is not possible. A person must first be changed, in order that his deeds may be changed. For if a person persists in what is evil, he cannot have good deeds, nor can he have evil deeds if he perseveres in what is good. Who is there who has been found to be good, since *Christ died for the ungodly?*[20] He found us all to be bad trees, but gave us *power to become children of God.*[21] So whoever is good today, that is, whoever is a good tree, has been found to be bad and made good.

If, when he comes, he wants to dig up the bad trees, who will remain who does not deserve to be dug up? But he comes to offer his mercy first, that he may then exercise judgement. To him it is said *I will sing of mercy and of justice; to you, O Lord, I will sing.*[22] He has given to believers remission of sins, he has not wished to look over their earlier accounts. He has given them remission of sins and made them good trees. He has put away his axe and given them security.[23] John speaks of this axe when he says *Even now the axe is lying at the root of the trees; every tree therefore that does not bear good fruit is cut down and thrown into the fire*[24]. The landowner in the Gospel warns about this axe when he says *For three years I have come looking for fruit on this fig tree, and still I find none. Cut it down! Why should it be wasting the soil?*[25] And the gardener pleads with him, saying *Sir, let it alone for one more year, until I dig around it and put manure on it. If it bears fruit next year, well and good; but if not, you can cut it down.*[26]

The Lord visited the human race as it were for three years, that is, during three periods. The first was before the giving of the Law, the second under the Law, and the third now, that is, during the time of grace. If he did not visit the human race before the Law was given, how can we explain Abel, Enoch, Noah, Abraham, Isaac or Jacob? He wanted to be called their Lord and he, to whom all nations belong, spoke as if he were the God of only three men, saying *I am the God of Abraham, the God of Isaac, and the God of Jacob*.[27] Had he not visited us in the time of the Law, he would not have been the giver of the Law itself. After the Law the landowner came again: he suffered, he died, he rose again, he gave the Holy Spirit, he caused the Gospel to be preached throughout the world, and still there were some trees that remained without fruit. There is still a part of the human race that refuses to correct itself.

So, since he must come, let us work so that he may find us bearing fruit. The digging of a ditch around the tree is a sign of humility, for every ditch is low. The manure is a sign of penitence, for what is dirtier than manure, and yet, if you use it well, what is more fruitful? So let everybody be a good tree: do not think that you have good fruit if you are still a bad tree. There is no good fruit except from good trees. Change your heart, and your deeds will change. Root out cupidity and plant love, *for as the love of money is a root of all kinds of evil*,[28] so love is the root of all that is good. (Saint Augustine)[29]

4. Monday

> *There were also many lepers in Israel in the time of the prophet Elisha, and none of them was cleansed except Naaman the Syrian.*[30]

These words of our Lord and Saviour are clearly meant to teach us and to encourage us to reverence for his divinity, showing that nobody is healed and freed from the disease of leprosy without having earnestly prayed for healing, for God's gifts are not given to those who are asleep, but to those who keep their eyes open. <> Why did the prophet not cure his brethren, his fellow-citizens, his companions, whereas he did heal foreigners who did not share with him his religion or the observance of the law? Was it not to show that God gives healing according to his free will, not because of the race of the person healed, and that God's gifts are obtained by prayer, not by anyone's having a natural right to them? Learn, therefore, the humility to ask for what you hope to obtain: the gifts of heaven do not come automatically to people who make difficulties.

This is a simple explanation which has a moral lesson to teach us; but this passage from the gospel also reveals something about sacramental grace. <> The Church is a people, gathered from among the gentiles, which previously had been leprous and unclean before it was washed in the mystical water of baptism. Once it had received that sacrament it was clean of all stains both in body and mind, and began to be a virgin without spot or wrinkle.[31] Naaman is rightly said to be a great man, in high favour with his master[32] and wonderful to look at, for he is a sign of the salvation of the nations that was to come about: accordingly, he was advised to look to the prophet for healing by a holy young girl[33] who had been captured by the enemy power after the strength of her own people had been broken, and he was healed, not by the power of an earthly king, but by the generosity of God's mercy. <>

When they heard this, all in the synagogue were filled with rage: they got up and drove him out of the town.[34] <> This also helps you to understand that Jesus underwent his bodily sufferings, not out of necessity, but because he willed to do so, and he was not captured by the Jews, but gave himself up to them. He was captured when he willed, he fell when he willed, he was crucified when he willed, and when he did not will it, he did not allow himself to be captured. Here he was on the top of a hill, about to be thrown off, and he came down again through the middle of the angry crowd, who must suddenly have changed their mind or have been overcome: the hour of his passion had not yet come.[35] <> You see that what he does here is a work of his divine power, just as his arrest was in accord with his will. How could he have been arrested by a few people, when a whole crowd was unable to capture him? He did not wish a large number of people to be involved in such a sacrilege. He wished blame to fall on those who brought him to the cross, and to be crucified by a few, but to die for the whole world. (Saint Ambrose)[36]

5. Tuesday

The kingdom of heaven may be compared to a king who wished to settle accounts with his slaves. When he began the reckoning, one who owed him ten thousand talents was brought to him; and, as he could not pay, his lord ordered him to be sold, together with his wife and children and all his possessions, and payment to be made. So the slave fell on his knees before him, saying, 'Have patience with me, and I will pay you everything.' And out of pity for him, the lord of that slave released him and forgave him the debt. But that same slave, as he went out, came upon one of his fellow slaves who owed him a hundred denarii; and seizing him by the throat, he said, 'Pay what you owe.' Then his fellow slave fell down and pleaded with him, 'Have patience with me, and I will pay you.' But he refused; then he went and threw him into prison until he would pay the debt.[37]

Do you see how great is the difference between sins against humans and sins against God? It is as great as the difference between a thousand talents and a hundred denarii, or rather much more. This is both because of the difference between those sinned against and because of the frequency of the sins. When a human being sees us we stop sinning and are ashamed to begin again; but God sees us every day, and yet we do not desist, but continue to take pleasure in sinning and to talk about it. Because of this, and also because of God's kindness to us and the honour he has shown us, such sins are the more wicked.

If you want to know how our sins against God can be compared to a thousand talents and more, I shall try to show you briefly. < > To do this, I shall speak first of the goodness of God. What are his kindnesses? He made us when we were not, and he made for our sake all that we can see, the sky, the sea, the earth, the air and everything in them, animals, plants and seeds – the boundless ocean of his works compels me to be brief. He breathed into us, alone of all the creatures on earth, a living soul, he planted Paradise for us, gave us a partner to help us, set us above all irrational creatures *and crowned* us *with glory and honour*.[38] Then, when we had grown ungrateful towards our benefactor, he counted us worthy of a greater gift.

Do not only remember the fact that he cast us out of Paradise, but also the prize that came to us because of this. After he had cast us out of Paradise and done all those good things for us, and had cared for us in so many ways, he sent his Son to those who had repaid his kindness with hatred, opened heaven to them and welcomed them to Paradise, adopting his proud enemies as his children. So now we may rightly exclaim *O the depth of the riches and wisdom and knowledge of God!*[39] He has given us baptism for the forgiveness of our sins and the remission of punishment, he has made us heirs of his kingdom, he has promised a thousand good things to those who live virtuously, he has stretched out his hand to us and poured his Spirit into our hearts. So how should we have behaved after receiving such good things? Even if we were to die every day for one who has loved us so much, would we recompense him as he deserves, or even pay back a small part of our debt? Not at all. <> Seeing, then, that this is how we ought to live, how in fact do we behave? Every day we insult him and disobey his laws. Do not be angry with me when I speak against sinners, for I am not only thinking of your sins, but of my own. (Saint John Chrysostom)[40]

6. Wednesday

'Do not think that I have come to abolish the law or the prophets; I have come not to abolish but to fulfil'.[41]

How is it that he did not abolish the law or the prophets, but fulfilled them? By his deeds he confirmed everything that had been said about him by the prophets, *so that on each occasion the evangelist says so that what had been spoken through the prophet... might be fulfilled:*[42] when he was born, when the children sang their wonderful hymn about him, when he sat on the ass and on many other occasions he fulfilled the prophets, all of whose prophecies would have remained unfulfilled if he had not come. As for the Law, he fulfilled it not in one way only but in a second and a third. Firstly, by never transgressing any of the commandments. <> Secondly, by obeying it on our behalf. It is a wonderful thing that he not only fulfilled the law for himself but, in his generosity, for us as well. <> And if you think carefully, you will discover another way, the third, in which he fulfilled the Law. What is that? By means of the new law that he was to give in the future. That was not a removal of the previous one, but rather an extension and fulfilment of it. His commandment against anger is a fulfilment of the commandment against murder[43] and a more secure defence against transgressions of it, and the same is true of all the others.

When he said those things he was naming the rewards that await those who live rightly, but now he names the punishments of those who do not. Then he said that the meek will inherit the earth; now that anybody who calls his brother or sister a fool will be liable to the hell of fire. Then he said that the pure in heart will see God; now that anybody who casts an impure glance is truly an adulterer. Then he called the peacemakers children of God; now he deters us with the threat *your accuser may hand you over to the judge*.[44] Having blessed those who mourn and those who are persecuted, he now holds out the prospect of damnation to those who do not walk by that path, promising that those who take the easy road will perish there. To me, *You cannot serve God and wealth*[45] means the same as *Blessed are the merciful*[46] and *Blessed are those who hunger... for righteousness*.[47] (Saint John Chrysostom)[48]

7. Thursday

If it is by the finger of God that I cast out the demons, then the kingdom of God has come to you.[49]

Nobody can hold a correct opinion about the Son who is deceived regarding the Spirit. If anybody thinks the Holy Spirit is small because he is called the finger of God, they will also think the Son is a small part of God because he is called God's right hand. <> But these things have been written so that we might refer them to the unity of the Trinity and believe what the Apostle says, that *the whole fullness of deity dwells bodily* in Christ,[50] and in the Father and in the Holy Spirit, and that just as there is one Godhead, so there is one divine operation. We can learn the same lesson from the Song of Moses. He had led the Jewish people through the sea, and confessed the operation of God, Father, Son and Holy Spirit, when he said *Your right hand, O Lord, glorious in power— your right hand, O Lord, shattered the enemy*[51] – here he confessed the Father and the Father's right hand, who is the Son. Then, so as not to overlook the Holy Spirit, he added *You blew with your wind, the sea covered them*,[52] which signified the unity of the Godhead, not inequality among the Trinity. You see, then, how the Holy Spirit worked with the Father and the Son, so that the waves might congeal in the middle of the sea and a wall of water might rise up to allow the Jews to pass, and then fall to drown the people of Egypt. Many people also think that the column of cloud went before the Jews by day and the column of fire by night that his people might be protected by the grace of the Spirit.

The apostle also declares that this work of God, at which the whole world is rightly astonished, did not take place without the work of the Spirit when he says the truth of the mystery of the Spirit went before them. He says *our ancestors were all under the cloud, and all passed through the sea, and all were baptized into Moses in the cloud and in the sea, and all ate the same spiritual food, and all drank the same spiritual drink.*[53] How could there be a foreshadowing of a sacrament without the work of the Holy Spirit, who is the source of all sacramental power? This is what the Apostle teaches when he says *But you were washed, you were sanctified, you were justified in the name of the Lord Jesus Christ and in the Spirit of our God.*[54] So you see that the Father works in the Son and the Son works in the Spirit, and so do not doubt that in the early books of the Bible mysteries were foreshadowed which Truth himself later declared to be true. For who can deny that he is at work in the Font, where we experience his work and his grace? So the Father sanctifies, the Son sanctifies and the Holy Spirit sanctifies, but there is one sanctification, for there is one baptism, and one grace of the sacrament. (Saint Ambrose)[55]

8. Friday

One of the scribes came near and heard them disputing with one another, and seeing that Jesus answered them well, he asked him, 'Which commandment is the first of all?'[56]

Matthew says[57] that the scribe asked his question to test Jesus, but Mark says the opposite: *When Jesus saw that he answered wisely, he said to him, 'You are not far from the kingdom of God.'*[58] The two gospel-writers are not contradicting each other here, but are very much in agreement, for Jesus was testing him at the beginning when he asked his question[59] and then, being pleased with the scribe's answer, he commended him. He did not commend him at the beginning, but only when he said that to love one's neighbour is *more important than all whole burnt offerings.*[60] Then he said, *You are not far from the kingdom*, because he looked beyond unimportant matters and grasped the beginning of virtue, from which all the other things spring, the Sabbath and everything else. And when he commended him, he did not praise him to the full, but so far only partially. To say *You are not far from the kingdom* is to imply that he still has some way to go, so as to encourage him to complete the journey. Why did the scribe begin by asking this question of Jesus? He was hoping to find some reason to correct him, because he was speaking of himself as God. What did Christ do? To show that the scribe had come for this purpose because he had no love, because he was overcome by jealousy and envy, he said *'You shall love the Lord your God:*[61] this is the first and great commandment, and the second is like it, *and you shall love your neighbour as yourself'.*[62] Why is the second like the first? Because it prepares the way for it, and loving the Lord our God depends on loving one another, for in loving one another we love the one who made us as we are, according to his image. Our natural love of one another does not arise from our love of God, but from loving one another we move on to give thanks to the one who made us and bestowed such countless gifts upon us, and thus, so far as we are able, we repay him for his great love. <> Having been asked about the first commandment, he brought in the second also, which is no less than it. The law says more than enough in speaking about this *with all the heart, and with all the under-*

standing, and with all the strength,[63] to bring love to its perfection, not permitting any limits that might lessen love towards God. Having called this the great commandment, the Lord added that it was the first, in order to introduce the second, which is bound up with it and cannot be separated from it. <> Love directed towards God is not true, if it does not go with love for one's neighbour. (from an anonymous Greek commentary)[64]

9. Saturday

He also told this parable to some who trusted in themselves that they were righteous and regarded others with contempt: 'Two men went up to the temple to pray, one a Pharisee and the other a tax collector. The Pharisee, standing by himself, was praying thus, "God, I thank you that I am not like other people: thieves, rogues, adulterers, or even like this tax collector. I fast twice a week; I give a tenth of all my income." But the tax collector, standing far off, would not even look up to heaven, but was beating his breast and saying, "God, be merciful to me, a sinner!" '[65]

The Lord has just told a parable to teach us to pray always and not to lose heart, ending with a warning that when the judge comes it will be difficult for him to find any faith on earth.[66] Now he at once adds another parable to show clearly that God does not judge the words in which we profess our faith, but the deeds by which we express it. Among these deeds the most important is humility. That is why earlier, when he had compared faith to a grain of mustard which is tiny but grows great,[67] he added as if by way of explanation *when you have done all that you were ordered to do, say, 'We are worthless slaves'.*[68] The proud, by contrast, when they do a little of what the Lord commands, and by no means everything, at once begin to trust in themselves that they are righteous and to regard the weak with contempt, and so when they pray they are not heard, for they are empty of faith. <>

There are four ways in which the arrogance of the proud manifests itself: either they think that the good they have comes from themselves, or, if they believe it has been given to them from above, they think they have received it as a reward for their merits, or they boast of things they do not have, or they despise everybody else and wish to be thought the only people who have what they have. It is clear that this Pharisee had the disease of boasting, since he went down from the Temple without being justified because he put himself above the publican who was praying there, as if he was the only person who deserved a reward for his good deeds. <> He was concerned to live temperately, to show mercy and to give thanks to God, but he took no care over humility. What is the use of guarding almost an entire city against the attacks of the enemy if one little opening is left for them to rush in?

I tell you, this man went down to his home justified rather than the other.[69] The publican was perfectly aware of his sinfulness, he wept over it, he confessed it and, if he went to the Temple an unjust man, he returned to his home justified: what confidence in God's pardon this offers to those who truly repent of their sins! <> The words of the proud Pharisee which, had he thought about them, should have made him humble, can offer us a model of humility which will raise us up. By considering the vices of people worse than himself and his own virtues he was lifted up to his own ruin; so we should be humbled and thus brought to glory, not only by the thought of our own laziness, but also by that of the virtues of others. (Saint Bede)[70]

NOTES

1. John 4:7-10
2. John 4:11

3. John 4:14
4. John 4:13
5. Ps 65:4
6. John 4:23
7. Ps 113:5-6
8. Ps 34:18
9. 1 Cor 3:17
10. *Commentary on John* 15, 12-15; 25; *PL* 35, 1514-1515; 1519-1520
11. John 2:24
12. John 2:23
13. John 2:25
14. John 3:3
15. Ex 16:14-16
16. 1 Cor 10:1-2
17. John 6:51
18. *Commentary on John* 11, 2-4; *PL* 35, 1474-1477
19. Matt 12:33
20. Rom 5:6
21. John 1:12
22. Ps 101:1
23. There is a pun in the Latin here, since the Latin word for 'axe' is *securis*.
24. Matt 3:10
25. Luke 13:7
26. Luke 13:8-9
27. Ex 3:14-15
28. 1 Tim 6:10
29. *Sermon on the Gospel* 72, 1-4; *PL* 38, 467-468
30. Luke 4:27
31. cf. Eph 5:27
32. 2 Kings 5:1
33. In Ambrose's interpretation, the young girl represents the people of Israel.
34. Luke 4:28-29
35. John 8:20

36. *Commentary on Luke* 4, 49-55; *PL* 15, 1710-1713
37. Matt 18:23-30
38. Ps 8:5
39. Rom 11:33
40. *Commentary on Matthew* 61, 1-2; *PG* 58, 589-590
41. Matt 5:17
42. Matt 4:14
43. Matt 5:21-22
44. Matt 5:25
45. Matt 6:24
46. Matt 5:7
47. Matt 5:6
48. *Commentary on Matthew* 16, 2-3; *PG* 57, 241-242
49. Luke 11:20
50. Col 2:9
51. Ex 15:6
52. Ex 15:10
53. 1 Cor 10:1-4
54. 1 Cor 6:11
55. *On the Holy Spirit* 3, 4; *PL* 16, 814-815
56. Mark 12:28
57. Matt 22:35
58. Mark 12:34
59. Matt 22:35
60. Mark 12:33
61. Mark 12:30
62. Mark 12:31
63. Mark 12:33
64. Cramer, J. A. *Catenae Graecorum Patrum* (Oxford, 1844), vol. 1, pp.403-404
65. Luke 18:9-13
66. Luke 18:1-8
67. Luke 17:6
68. Luke 17:10
69. Luke 18:14
70. *Commentary on Luke* 5, 18; *PL* 92, 551-553

5

THE FOURTH WEEK OF LENT

1. Sunday Year A

The Lord came, and what did he do? He drew our attention to a great mystery. *He spat on the ground and made mud with the saliva,*[1] because *the Word became flesh,*[2] and anointed the blind man's eyes. He was anointed, but could not yet see. Jesus sent him to the pool called Siloam. The evangelist wanted to emphasize to us the importance of the name of this pool, and so he said *which means Sent.*[3] You already know who it was that was *sent,* for if he had not been *sent,* none of us would have been freed from the sentence our sins deserve.[4] So he washed his eyes in the pool called *Sent,* that is, he was baptized in Christ. So if Jesus enlightened him when in some sense he baptized him in himself, perhaps he was making him a catechumen when he anointed him. There are so many ways in which the depths of this great sacrament can be described and explained, but let this be enough for your Charity: what you have heard is a great mystery. Ask a person 'Are you a Christian?', and if he is a pagan or a Jew he will reply 'I am not'. But if he answers 'I am', you will go on to ask, 'Are you a catechumen, or one of the faithful?' If he answers 'a Catechumen', he is anointed but not yet washed. But how has he been anointed? <> Ask him who he believes in. Because he is a catechumen, he will say 'in Christ'. Now at this moment I am speaking both to catechumens and to the faithful. What did I say about the mud and the saliva? That *the Word became flesh.*[5] The catechumens hear these words, but it is not enough that they have been anointed:[6] they must hurry to the washing of baptism if they seek to be enlightened. <>

Jesus himself gave the reason why that man had been born

blind when he said *Neither this man nor his parents sinned; he was born blind so that God's works might be revealed in him.*[7] Then what follows? *I must work the works of him who sent me.* You see, Jesus is the one who was *sent*, the one in whom the blind man washed his face. And see what he said: *I must work the works of him who sent me while it is day.*[8] Remember that he gives all glory to the one from whom he comes, for the Father has a Son who owes his origin to him, but the Father owes his origin to nobody. But Lord, why did you say *while it is day*? Listen to the reason. *Night is coming when no one can work.*[9] <> Listen to what the day is, and then you will understand what night is. <> *As long as I am in this world, I am the light of the world.*[10] You see – he is the Day. Let the blind man wash his eyes in the Day, that he may see the day. *As long as I am in the world*, he says, *I am the light of the world.* <>

What, then, are we to say of that night in which no one can work? When will it be? It will be the night of the wicked, of those to whom at the end will be said <> *Bind him hand and foot, and throw him into the outer darkness.*[11] So let us work while we are alive, so that we are not overtaken by that night in which no one can work. Now is the time for *faith working through love,*[12] and if we work now, the Day is here, Christ is here. Listen to his promise, and do not imagine that he is absent: *Remember, I am with you always.*[13] <> But after the resurrection of the living and the dead, when he has said to those at his right hand, *Come, you that are blessed by my Father, inherit the kingdom,*[14] and to those at his left, *Depart from me into the eternal fire prepared for the devil and his angels,*[15] there will be the night when no one can work, but only receive payment for his work. (Saint Augustine)[16]

2. Sunday Year B

And this is the judgment, that the light has come into the world, and people loved darkness rather than light because their deeds were evil.[17]

What does this mean? Who are they whose deeds were good? Did you not come to justify the wicked? And yet *people loved darkness rather than light*.[18] There is the point: many loved their sins, and many confessed their sins, for whoever confesses his sins and accuses himself of sin is already working with God. God accuses you of sin, and if you also accuse yourself, you are united with God. A man and a sinner are, as it were, two things. What you hear spoken of as 'man' is what God has made; what is called 'sinner' is what man has made. Do away with what you have made, that God may save what he has made. You must hate your own work in yourself that you may love God's work in you.

Once your deeds begin to displease you, your good deeds begin, for you are reproaching your evil deeds. The beginning of good deeds is the confession of evil deeds. You do what is true, and you come to the light. What does it mean to say that you do what is true? You do not praise yourself, you do not flatter yourself, you do not admire yourself; you do not say 'I am just' when you are wicked: thus you begin to do what is true. You come to the light that it may be clearly seen that your deeds have been done in God, for your very sin which displeases you would not displease you if God's light were not shining on you and his truth were not showing you the truth. But a person who loves his sin even after being warned hates the light that warns him and flees from it, that he may not be accused of the bad deeds he loves to do. One who does what is true accuses his evil deeds within himself: he does not spare himself, he does not pardon himself, so that God may pardon him, and he comes to the Light, to whom he gives thanks for showing him what to hate in himself. He says to God *Hide your face from my sins*,[19] and what can this mean, except what he also says: *For I know my transgressions, and my sin is ever before me*?[20]

Put before your own face what you do not want to be before the face of God. But if you put your sin behind you, God will put it back before your eyes, and that will be when

69

there is no time left for penitence to bear fruit. Hurry, my brothers and sisters, so that the darkness does not overcome you. Stay awake for your own salvation, keep vigil while there is still time. Let nobody be slow in coming to God's temple, in doing the work of God. Let nobody be drawn away from continual prayer, let nobody be deceived into abandoning a life of devotion. Stay awake while it is day: the daylight is bright, for Christ is the day. He is ready to forgive, but only those who confess. (Saint Augustine)[21]

3. Sunday Year C

'Father, I have sinned against heaven and before you; I am no longer worthy to be called your son.'[22]

We must be careful not to delay in seeking reconciliation, for the Father does not delay. He is easily reconciled to those who earnestly ask for it. So let us discover how one would pray to the Father for reconciliation. *Father*, says the son: how merciful and loving the Father is who, although he has been sinned against, accepts to be called 'father'. *Father*, he says, *I have sinned against heaven and before you*. This is above all a confession to the creator of all things, the Lord of mercy, the judge of our guilt. Although God knows all things, he still waits to hear the words of your confession, for *one confesses with the mouth*.[23] A person who acknowledges his blame exonerates himself by that very fact, and if we confess before we are accused we avert the anger of our accuser. *The just man accuses himself as he begins to speak.*[24] It would be futile for you to try to hide from the One who is never deceived, and there is no danger in admitting what you know he already knows. Rather confess so that Christ, our *advocate with the Father*,[25] may intervene on your behalf, the Church may pray and the people weep for you. Do not be afraid to ask. Your advocate promises pardon, your protector promises his grace, the Lord who teaches us about the love of the Father promises you reconciliation. Believe, because it is true, and follow his teaching, for that is virtuous. He has a reason to plead for you: he does not wish to have died for you in vain. The Father has a reason for forgiving you, for what the Son desires the Father desires also. < >

Rise up, then, and run to the church: here you will find the Father, the Son and the Holy Spirit. He can hear you discussing with yourself in the secret places of your mind, and he is running to meet you. While you are still a long way off, he sees you and runs towards you. He sees into your heart and runs, in case anybody should come between you and him, and he embraces you. In his running there is foreknowledge, in his embrace mercy and love like that of a father. He puts his arms round you to lift you up from where you are lying weighed down with sins and turns your face, which is looking towards the earth, towards the sky so that it may look for its maker. Christ puts his arms around you to take away the yoke of slavery and put his easy yoke around your neck.[26] Do you not think he put his arms around John when he rested with his head bowed on Jesus' breast? It was thus that John saw the Word with God, when Jesus raised his face to look upwards. He puts his arms round us when he says *Come to me, all you that are weary and are carrying heavy burdens, and I will give you rest. Take my yoke upon you.*[27] That is how he embraces you, if you turn to him and are converted. <> (Saint Ambrose)[28]

4. Monday

When the two days were over, he went from that place to Galilee (for Jesus himself had testified that a prophet has no honour in the prophet's own country).[29]

Jesus did not leave Samaria because he had no honour there, for Samaria was not his own country, but Galilee. Having left Samaria so quickly and come to Galilee where he had been brought up, how can he have *testified that a prophet has no honour in the prophet's own country*? Those words would have seemed more suitable if he had stayed in Samaria and refused to go to Galilee. <> The evangelist knew what he was saying better than I, and saw the truth better than I, for he drank in the truth at the breast of the Lord. He is John the evangelist, who was chosen above all the other disciples to recline on the breast of the Lord, and whom the Lord, who owed love to all, nevertheless loved more than all others. Is it likely, then, that he would be wrong and I right? No: if I am truly reverent I should listen obediently to his words so that I may come to understand his meaning. <>

He came back, then, to this town in Galilee. *Now there was a royal official whose son lay ill in Capernaum. When he heard that Jesus had come from Judaea to Galilee, he went and begged him to come down and heal his son, for he was at the point of death.*[30] Did the man who made this prayer not believe? <> Ask the Lord what he thought of him, for he replied to his entreaty with the words *Unless you see signs and wonders you will not believe*[31] to show that this was a man of lukewarm or cool faith, or of no faith at all, somebody who was using his child's sickness to discover what sort of person Christ was, who he was, and what he could do. For we have heard his prayer, but we have not seen into his faithless heart, but the Lord who both heard his words and looked into his heart made clear, and then the evangelist shows by his story, that when the official wanted the Lord to come to his house and heal his son, he did not yet believe.

The official learned that his son had recovered and compared the time this happened with the time when Jesus spoke to him, and *so he himself believed, along with his whole household:*[32] this shows that when he asked Jesus to come to his house, he did not yet believe. But the Samaritans had not waited for a sign: they had believed his word alone, while Jesus' own townsfolk deserved the reproach *Unless you see signs and wonders you will not believe*, and even after so great a miracle nobody believed except the official and his household.

Although Thomas, who desired to put his fingers into the Lord's wounds, was one of the Twelve, the chosen and holy ones, nevertheless the Lord reproached him and this royal official in the same way, saying to this man *Unless you see signs and wonders you will not believe*, and to Thomas *Have you believed because you have seen me?*[33] He had come to the Galileans after the Samaritans, who had believed in his words without his performing any miracles among them, and he had left them quickly in assurance that their faith was firm, although his divine presence had not left them. So when the Lord said to Thomas *Reach out your hand and put it in my side. Do not doubt but believe*,[34] and when Thomas exclaimed *My Lord and my God!*[35] Jesus reproached him and said *Have you believed because you have seen me?*[36] Why does he say that, if not because *a prophet has no honour in the prophet's own country*? And because this prophet has honour among people other than his own, what follows? Blessed are those who have not seen and yet have come to believe.[37] The Lord is speaking here of us: we are the ones to whom in his generosity he has given the faith that he praises here. Those who crucified him saw him and touched him, and openly a few of them believed. We have neither seen nor touched him, but only heard of him, and we have believed. May the blessedness he has promised come to perfection in us. (Saint Augustine)[38]

5. Tuesday

Jesus found in the age of the man he cured a number signifying his sickness: he *had been ill for thirty-eight years*.[39] Why this number is more appropriate for sickness will take a little explanation. <> The number forty is recommended to us very often in Holy Scripture as a sacred number which in a way signifies perfection. <> Fasting is consecrated with this number, for Moses fasted forty days,[40] and so did Elijah,[41] and our

Lord and saviour Jesus Christ completed the same number of days of fasting.[42] Moses stands for the Law, Elijah for the Prophets, and the Lord for the Gospel. So these three appeared on the mountain when Jesus showed himself to his disciples with his face and clothing radiant.[43] He stood between Moses and Elijah, as if to signify that both the Law and the Prophets witness to the Gospel. So the number forty is recommended to us by fasting in the Law, the Prophets and the Gospel. The great fast that binds everybody is the fast from sins and the forbidden pleasures of the world: this is a perfect fast, *training us to renounce impiety and worldly passions, and in the present age to live lives that are self-controlled, upright, and godly.*[44] What reward does the Apostle promise for such a fast? He goes on to say *while we wait for the blessed hope and the manifestation of the glory of our great God and Saviour, Jesus Christ.*[45] So in this world we keep the fast of forty days when we live well, abstaining from sins and forbidden pleasures.

The number forty signifies a certain perfection in good deeds, which are done best in a certain abstinence from the forbidden pleasures of the world, that is, in a complete fast. How does love come about? By the grace of God, by the Holy Spirit. We cannot have it by ourselves as if it were our own creation. It is a gift of God, and a great gift, *because God's love has been poured into our hearts through the Holy Spirit that has been given to us.*[46] So love fulfils the law, and the saying *love is the fulfilling of the law*[47] is very true. Let us seek for this love, since the Lord recommends it to us.

Remember what I have been speaking about: I want to explain the number thirty-eight in connection with the sick man in the Gospel, and why that is a number more appropriate to sickness than to health.

Love fulfils the law. The number forty applies to the fulfilment of the law in every good deed, while we have been given two commandments of love. The commandments of love given us by the Lord are two: *You shall love the Lord your God with all your heart, and with all your soul, and with all your*

The Fourth Week of Lent

mind and you shall love your neighbour as yourself. On these two commandments hang all the law and the prophets.[48] So it was suitable that the widow who gave all that she had put two coins into God's treasury,[49] and that the inn-keeper was given two coins for the healing of the man wounded by thieves,[50] and that Jesus spent two days among the Samaritans, to confirm them in love.[51] When anything good is signified in the scriptures, and especially love with its two aspects, the number two is used. So if the number forty stands for the fulfilment of the law and the law is not fulfilled except through the twofold commandment of love, why be surprised if a man who was two short of forty was said to be sick? (Saint Augustine)[52]

6. Wednesday

My Father is still working, and I also am working.[53]

Was the Scripture lying, then, when it said that God *rested on the seventh day from all the work that he had done?*[54] And can Jesus be contradicting these words of Scripture which have been handed down through the ministry of Moses when he himself says to the Jews *If you believed Moses, you would believe me, for he wrote about me?*[55] Did not Moses intend to teach us something when he said that God rested on the seventh day?[56] God had not grown tired while making creation: he did not need to rest as a human would. Nonetheless it is true that God *rested on the seventh day from all the work that he had done*, and what Jesus says, *My Father is still working, and I also am working*, is also true. But who can explain in words <> how God works in rest and rests as he works? <> Perhaps we can say that by his rest on the seventh day God was giving us a great and mysterious sign of our Lord and Saviour Jesus Christ, who said *My Father is still working, and I also am working*, for the Lord Jesus is God as well. He is the Word of God, and you know that *In the beginning was the Word*, not any

75

word, but *the Word was God*,[57] and *all things came into being through him*:[58] perhaps the scripture means that it is he who will rest on the seventh day from all the work that he has done.

Read the Gospel and you will see the work that Jesus has done. He brought about our salvation on the cross, so that all the predictions of the prophets were fulfilled in him. He was crowned with thorns and hung on the tree, he said *I am thirsty*,[59] he received vinegar on a sponge to fulfil the Psalm *for my thirst they gave me vinegar to drink*.[60] When all his work was done, on the sixth day of the week he bowed his head and gave up his spirit, and on the sabbath he rested in the tomb from all the work that he had done. It is as if he were saying to the Jews 'Why do you expect me not to work on the sabbath? You were commanded to observe the sabbath day as a sign of me. Think of the works of God: I was there when they came into being, they all came into being through me. <> *My Father is still working*. My Father made the light, but in order that there might be light, he spoke: he worked through his Word. I was his word, and I am the Word. It was through me that the world was made in those works, and by me that the world is governed today. My Father worked then when he made the world, and he works now in governing the world: therefore when he made it he made it through me, and when he governs it he does so through me.' Thus he spoke, but to whom? To the deaf, the blind, the lame, the sick, who did not recognise their physician and behaved foolishly, seeking to kill him as if they had lost their minds. (Saint Augustine)[61]

7. Thursday

You sent messengers to John, and he testified to the truth....
He was a burning and shining lamp...[62]

Imagine that it is night-time: you look at a lamp and marvel at it, but the lamp reminds you that there is a sun for you to rejoice in, and its flame in the night encourages you to wait for the day. It is not because there was no need for the human testimony of John – for why would he have been sent if there had been no need? – but in order that humankind might not remain in the lamplight and think that it was enough for us, that the Lord neither says that that lamp was unnecessary nor says that you ought to remain in the lamplight.

We find another testimony in Scripture: there God bore witness to his Son, and in Scripture the Jews placed their hope, that is, in the Law that had been given them by the ministry of God's servant, Moses. *You search the scriptures because you think that in them you have eternal life; and it is they that testify on my behalf. Yet you refuse to come to me to have life.*[63] Why do you think you have eternal life in the Scriptures? Ask the Scriptures to whom they bear testimony, and you will understand what eternal life is. Since because of Moses they wanted to reject Christ as an enemy of the commandments and institutions of Moses, he proves them wrong again by use, as it were, of another lamp.

All humans are lamps, since they can be lit and extinguished: they are lamps when luminous with wisdom and warm with the fire of the Spirit, and if their flame has been extinguished they smell. God's servants remain as good lamps by the oil of his mercy, not by their own strength, for it is the freely-given grace of God that is the oil in those lamps. <> Every prophecy before the coming of the Lord is a lamp, as the apostle Peter says, *So we have the prophetic message more fully confirmed. You will do well to be attentive to this as to a lamp shining in a dark place, until the day dawns and the morning star rises in your hearts.*[64] So the prophets are lamps, and every prophecy is a great lamp. What of the Apostles? Are they not lamps? Certainly they are. Only Christ is not a lamp, for he cannot be lit and extinguished since *just as the Father has life in himself, so he has granted the Son also to have life in himself.*[65] So the Apostles are lamps as well, and they give thanks because they have been lit with the light of Truth, they are warm with the Spirit of love, and their oil is the grace of God. If they were not lamps, the Lord would not have said to them *You are the light of the world.*[66] <> So Moses testified to Christ, John the Baptist testified to Christ, the other prophets and apostles testified to Christ. Above all these testimonies he places the testimony of his own works, because through those none other than God was testifying to his own Son. And God testifies to his Son in another way: through the Son he makes the Son known, and he makes himself known as well. Anybody who comes to the Son will need no lamps: he will dig deep and build his house upon the Rock. (Saint Augustine)[67]

8. Friday

> *After this Jesus went about in Galilee. He did not wish to go about in Judaea because the Jews were looking for an opportunity to kill him. Now the Jewish festival of Booths was near.*[68]

Everything that was said to the ancient people of Israel in all the writings concerned with the holy Law about what they should do regarding sacrifices, priesthood, feastdays and everything else connected with the worship of God, all these sayings and commandments are shadows of what was to come in the future. What was that? Everything that was fulfilled in Christ. <> If all these things were a shadow of what is to come, so was the festival of Booths. Of what future thing was it a shadow? This was the festival of tents, kept because the people lived in tents on their journey through the desert to the promised land after they had been set free from Egypt. <>

We have been led out of Egypt, where we were slaves of the devil as if he were Pharaoh, making works of clay[69] in our earthly desires, and having great trouble with them. Christ called to us as if we were making bricks, *Come to me, all you that are weary and are carrying heavy burdens, and I will give you rest.*[70] We were led out from there and passed through baptism as if through the Red Sea, red because its water was made holy by the blood of Christ, and all the enemies who pursued us were killed, that is, all our sins were forgiven. So now, before we come to the promised land, that is, the eternal kingdom, we are in tents in the desert. <> A person dwells in tents when he understands that he is a pilgrim in this world: a person knows himself to be a pilgrim when he feels within himself a desire for his homeland.

Since, therefore, the body of Christ[71] is in tents, Christ himself is in tents. At the time of the Exodus this was not visibly so, but in a hidden way, for the light was still obscured by a shadow: when the light came, the shadow was removed. Christ was there in secret at the festival of Booths, he was hidden. But now that these mysteries have been made plain, we know that we are journeying through the desert, because we are in this world, a thirsty path with no water. Let us thirst that we may be satisfied, for *Blessed are those who hunger and thirst for righteousness, for they will be filled,*[72] and our thirst will be slaked in the desert from the rock, the rock that was Christ,[73] struck with a rod that water might gush forth. The rock was struck twice before it gushed[74] because the cross is made of two pieces of wood. So all these things which happened in an image are made plain in us, and what is said of the Lord is not in vain: *he also went to the festival, not publicly but, as it were, in secret.*[75] These words *in secret* also have a hidden meaning, for this day of the feast was a sign of the journey that the members of Christ were to make in the future. (Saint Augustine)[76]

9. Saturday

Then the temple police went back to the chief priests and Pharisees, who asked them, 'Why did you not arrest him?'[77]

Nothing is clearer or more simple than the truth, provided we are not living evil lives, and nothing is more difficult if we are in sin. See how the Pharisees and the scribes, who had a certain reputation for wisdom, continually accompanied Christ in order to trick him, even though they had seen his miracles and had read the scriptures: they gained nothing from all this, but rather were harmed by it. On the other hand the police, who had none of the things to boast about that the Pharisees had, had been won over by one speech of Jesus, and although they had come to capture him, they went away captivated by the wonder of what they had witnessed. It is not only their wisdom that deserves admiration, and the fact that they had no need of miracles but were drawn solely by his teaching, <> but also the boldness with which they spoke to those who had sent them, to the Pharisees who were Christ's enemies and doing everything they could against him.

The fact that they came back shows far greater courage than if they had remained, for had they stayed they would not have had to face the Pharisees' anger, but in fact they showed greater boldness and became heralds of the wisdom of Christ. They did not say 'We were unable to because of the crowd, which is listening to him as to a prophet', but *Never has anyone spoken like this*.[78] <> These are the words of people who are not only amazed at Jesus, but are also accusing the Pharisees for sending them to bind him to whom they should have listened. They had not heard him speak at length, but only briefly, for when a person's mind is sincere, there is no need for many words: such is the power of the truth.

And what of the Pharisees? They should have been ashamed, but their reaction is quite the reverse, and they accuse the police in their turn, saying *Surely you have not been deceived too, have you?*[79] <> What sense does it make, after Nicodemus has said *Our law does not judge people*[80] to reply *Surely you are not also from Galilee, are you?*[81] What they should have done was prove that they had a good reason for sending people to summon him without having spoken with him first, but instead they answered in a still ruder and more angry tone, *Search and you will see that no prophet is to arise from Galilee*.[82] What had the man said? Had he claimed that Jesus was a prophet? No: he said that a person should not be killed without a trial, but they answered him arrogantly, as though he knew nothing of the Law, as if to say 'go and find out', for that is what *Search and you will see* means.

And what of Christ? Since they were constantly talking about Galilee and the prophet, he set them free from their mistaken opinions and revealed that he was not one of the prophets, but the Lord of the world, with the words *I am the Light of the World*.[83] (Saint John Chrysostom)[84]

NOTES

1. John 9:6
2. John 1:14: Augustine sees the mixture of saliva with mud as a sign of the mixture of divinity and humanity in the Incarnation.
3. John 9:7
4. Augustine plays on the words *missus* ('sent') and *dimissus* ('forgiven').
5. John 1:14
6. Catechumens are anointed early in the catechumenate, as they begin to learn about the Word made flesh. Like the anointing of the man born blind, this is only the beginning of a process of illumination.
7. John 9:3
8. John 9:4
9. John 9:4
10. John 9:5
11. Matt 22:13
12. Gal 5:6
13. Matt 28:20
14. Matt 25:34

15. Matt 25:41
16. *Commentary on John* 44, 2-6; *PL* 35, 1714-1716
17. John 3:19
18. John 3:19
19. Ps 51:9
20. Ps 51:3
21. *Commentary on John* 12, 13-14; *PL* 35, 1491
22. Luke 15:21
23. Rom 10:10
24. cf. Prov 18:17
25. 1 John 2:1
26. cf. Matt 11:29-30
27. Matt 11:28-29
28. *Commentary on Luke* 7, 224-230; *PL* 15, 1849-1851
29. John 4:43-44
30. John 4:46-47
31. John 4:48
32. John 4:53
33. John 20:29
34. John 20:27
35. John 20:28
36. John 20:29
37. John 20:29
38. *Commentary on John* 16, 1-4; *PL* 35, 1523-1525
39. John 5:5
40. Ex 34:28
41. 1 Kings 19:8
42. Matt 4:2
43. Matt 17:1-3
44. Titus 2:12
45. Titus 2:13
46. Rom 5:5
47. Rom 13:10
48. Matt 22:37;39-40
49. Luke 21:2
50. Luke 10:35

51. John 4:40
52. *Commentary on John* 17, 4-6; *PL* 35, 1529-1531
53. John 5:17
54. Gen 2:2
55. John 5:46
56. In Augustine's day, Moses was thought to have been the author of the entire Pentateuch.
57. John 1:1
58. John 1:3
59. John 19:28
60. Ps 69:21
61. *Commentary on John* 17, 14-15; *PL* 35, 1534-1535
62. John 5:33-35
63. John 5:39
64. 2 Pet 1:19
65. John 5:26
66. Matt 5:14
67. *Commentary on John* 23, 2-4; *PL* 35, 1582-1584
68. John 7:1-2
69. cf. Ex 5:7-19
70. Matt 11:28
71. i.e. the Church.
72. Matt 5:6
73. cf. 1 Cor 10:4
74. cf. Num 20:11
75. John 7:10
76. *Commentary on John* 28, 9; *PL* 35, 1626-1627
77. John 7:45
78. John 7:46
79. John 7:47
80. John 7:51
81. John 7:52
82. John 7:52
83. John 8:12
84. *Commentary on John* 52, 1-2: *PG* 59, 287-288

6

THE FIFTH WEEK OF LENT

1. Sunday Year A

Then Jesus told them plainly, 'Lazarus is dead. For your sake I am glad I was not there, so that you may believe. But let us go to him.'[1]

We read in the gospel that the Lord raised three people from the dead, and perhaps this is not without significance. The deeds of the Lord are not only deeds, but signs. So if they are signs, as well as arousing our wonder, they must have a meaning, and sometimes to find their meaning is harder than reading or hearing about them. As the Gospel was being read, we heard in amazement how Lazarus came back to life, as if this great miracle were being acted out before our eyes. If we think about works of Christ that are more wonderful than this, everybody who believes rises again. <>

So <> we can understand that the three dead people whom the Lord raised in the flesh teach us by signs and images about the resurrections of souls which come about through faith: he raised the daughter of the leader of the synagogue when she was still lying in her house; he raised the widow's young son who had been carried outside the gates of the city; he raised Lazarus after he had been in the tomb four days. Let us each look into our souls: if our soul sins, it dies, for sin is the death of the soul. But sometimes it sins by thought. If evil has pleased you and you have consented to it, you have sinned: that consent has killed you, but by an inner death, since your evil thought has not yet become an act. The Lord raised the girl who had not yet been carried out through the gates but lay dead indoors like a hidden sin, to show that he raises such souls.

But if you have not only consented to evil pleasure, but also done an evil deed, you have, as it were, carried the dead outside the gate: you are the dead man who has been carried out. However, the Lord healed him too and gave him back to his widowed mother.

If you have sinned, repent and the Lord will raise you, and give you back to your mother the Church.

The third dead person is Lazarus. This is a terrible kind of death, known as evil habit, since it is one thing to sin and another to make a habit of sin. Whoever sins and corrects himself at once comes quickly back to life: not being entrapped by habit, he is not buried. But one who sins habitually is buried, and is fitly called 'stinking' since he begins to have a bad reputation like an evil smell. Such are all who are accustomed to sin and abandoned in their morals. You say to them 'do not do it'. When do they listen to you, covered as they are with the earth, rotten and corrupt, weighed down with the load of habit? But the power of Christ is strong enough to raise even them.

I have known and seen, and see every day people who change the most evil habits and live better lives than those who rebuked them. <> We see many, we know many: let nobody despair, and nobody be presumptuous, for both despair and presumption are evil. Do not despair, but turn to the one on whom you must presume. (Saint Augustine)[2]

2. Sunday Year B

The hour has come for the Son of Man to be glorified. Very truly, I tell you, unless a grain of wheat falls into the earth and dies, it remains just a single grain; but if it dies, it bears much fruit. Those who love their life lose it, and those who hate their life in this world will keep it for eternal life.[3]

It is not enough for me merely to be amazed by these words: I am commanded to follow their teaching. Then, by the words that come next, *whoever serves me must follow me, and where I am, there will my servant be also*,[4] I am inspired to despise this world, and this life, however long it lasts, seems no more than a puff of smoke: because I love what is eternal, all temporal things seem worthless to me, and again I hear the voice of my Lord himself, who has called me with those words from my own weakness to his strength.

Let the man who desires to follow hear what follows. Perhaps a terrible hour arrives, with the choice of either doing wickedness or undergoing suffering, and trouble afflicts the weak soul: <> put the will of God before your own will. Then listen to the next words of your creator and master who made you and, in order to teach you, became what he made: for he who made man became a man, but remained God, unchangeable, and changed man into something better. Hear, then, what he says after *my soul is troubled*: he says *And what should I say – 'Father, save me from this hour'? No, it is for this reason that I have come to this hour. Father, glorify your name.*[5] He has taught you what to think, what to say, whom to pray to, in whom to hope, whose sure and divine will to put before your own weak, human will. Do not imagine that he has come down from his lofty state because he wants you to rise from your humble condition. He consented to be tempted by the devil, by whom he would not have been tempted had he not so wished, just as he would not have suffered had he not so wished, and he gave to the devil the reply that you must give when you are tempted. He was tempted, but not in danger, to teach you when you are in temptation and in danger to answer the tempter and not to follow him, but to escape the danger of temptation. Just as here he says *Now my soul is troubled*, so when he says *I am deeply grieved, even to death* and *My Father, if it is possible, let this cup pass from me*,[6] he has taken on himself human weakness in order to teach those who are similarly grieved and troubled to say what follows: *yet not what I want but what you want.*[7]

Human beings are led from the human to the divine when

they place the will of God above the will of man. What does he mean by *glorify your name*?[8] Surely, in his passion and resurrection. And for the Father to glorify the Son surely means that he glorifies his name also in his servants when they undergo similar sufferings. So it is written that he said about Peter *someone else will fasten a belt around you and take you where you do not wish to go*,[9] and *He said this to indicate the kind of death by which he would glorify God*.[10] So God glorified his name in Peter too, since that is how he glorifies Christ in his members. (Saint Augustine)[11]

3. Sunday Year C

> *The scribes and the Pharisees brought a woman who had been caught in adultery; and making her stand before all of them, they said to him, 'Teacher, this woman was caught in the very act of committing adultery. Now in the law Moses commanded us to stone such women. Now what do you say?' They said this to test him, so that they might have some charge to bring against him.*[12]

Because the law ordered adulterers to be stoned, and the law could not command something unjust, if anybody spoke against the commandment of the law, he would be shown to be unjust. <> So how did the Lord Jesus reply? <> He did not say 'she should not be stoned', lest he might seem to be contradicting the law. Even less would it have been right for him to say 'let her be stoned', since he came to seek out and to save the lost.[13] So what reply did he give? See how full he is of justice, of kindness and of truth: *Let anyone among you who is without sin be the first to throw a stone at her*.[14] That is the reply of Wisdom! How did he bring them back to themselves? They were casting calumnies outside themselves, without looking into themselves: they saw the adulteress, but they did not look at themselves. They were breakers of the law, for they wanted the law to be fulfilled, and they tried to bring this about by defamation, rather than by condemning adultery by their own chastity.

Jews, Pharisees, doctors of the Law, you have heard the guardian of the law, but you have not yet understood the words of the Legislator. What else did he wish to indicate by writing on the ground with his finger? The Law was written by the finger of God, but because of the hard of heart it was written in stone. Now the Lord was writing on the ground because he wanted to gather some fruit.[15] You have it from him that the law should be fulfilled and the adulteress stoned, but should the law be fulfilled in her punishment by people who deserve to be punished themselves? Let each of you think about this: enter into yourself, go up to the court of justice that is your own mind, stand before your conscience, make yourself confess. You know who you are, since no *human being knows what is truly human except the human spirit that is within.*[16] Anybody who examines himself finds that he is a sinner. Yes, it is true. So either let her go, or undergo the penalty of the law yourself, together with her. If Jesus were to say 'she should not be stoned', he would be shown up as unjust; if he were to say 'let her be stoned', he would seem unkind: let him say what is right for one who is both kind and just: *Let anyone among you who is without sin be the first to throw a stone at her.* This is the voice of Justice: let the sinner be punished, but not by sinners; let the law be fulfilled, but not by breakers of the law. This is the voice of Justice, and those who heard him, as if struck by a huge weapon, looked into themselves and found themselves guilty, and *they went away, one by one.*[17] Two remained, the pitiful woman and Pity himself. And once the Lord had struck them with the weapon of Justice, he did not consider it right to watch their downfall, but turned away from them and *once again he... wrote on the ground.*[18] (Saint Augustine)[19]

4. Monday

When there was nobody left except the woman, as everybody else was walking away, Jesus raised his eyes to her. We have heard the words of Justice: let us now listen to the words of Mercy. I think the woman must have been even more afraid when she heard the Lord say *Let anyone among you who is without sin be the first to throw a stone at her.*[20] Because of his words, her accusers examined themselves, and by their departure they confessed their guilt, leaving the woman with her great sin alone with him who was without sin. Since she had heard him say *Let anyone among you who is without sin be the first to throw a stone at her*, she expected to be punished by him in whom no sin could be found. But he, who had driven away her enemies with the tongue of Justice, raised to her the eyes of Mercy and asked *Has no one condemned you?*[21] She replied *No one, sir*, and he said 'I, from whom perhaps you feared condemnation because you found no sin in me, *Neither do I condemn you'*.

What is this, Lord? Are you in favour of sin? Certainly not. Listen to what follows: *Go your way, and from now on do not sin again.*[22] So the Lord did condemn, but he condemned the sin, not the sinner. If he had been in favour of sin, he would have said 'Neither do I condemn you: go and live as you please. Be certain that I set you free: however much you sin, I will free you from every punishment even in the underworld and from the torturers of hell'. But that was not what he said. Let those who love the Lord's mercy and fear his truth take notice. Yes, *Good and upright is the Lord:*[23] you love him because he is good: fear him because he is upright. <> The Lord is kind, the Lord is slow to anger, the Lord is merciful, but the Lord is also just, the Lord is truthful. <>

Human beings run a double risk, both in confidence and in despair, which are opposite realities, opposite feelings. A person is deceived by hope who misunderstands God and says 'The Lord is good, the Lord is merciful, I shall do as I please, as I desire, I shall give rein to my appetites, I shall fulfil the longings of my soul. Why? Because God is merciful, God is good, God is kind'. Such people are in danger because of their hope.

On the other hand, those who have fallen into grave sins and think that even if they repent they cannot be forgiven, and so decide that they are without any doubt destined to be damned, say to themselves in desperation 'We are damned already, so why should we not do as we wish?' They are like gladiators destined to die by the sword. That is why people without hope are so dangerous: they have nothing left to fear, and so they are to be feared themselves. Desperation ruins them, while hope ruins the others. <> To those in danger because of despair he says 'on the day when the wicked turn from their sin, I shall forget all their iniquities'.[24] To those in danger because of despair he offers the haven of forgiveness; because of those who are in danger through hope and think they have plenty of time, he has made the day of death uncertain. You do not know when the last day will come. Are you ungrateful because you have today in which to amend your life? So Jesus says to the woman *'Neither do I condemn you*, but now that you need have no anxiety about the past, be careful for the future. *Neither do I condemn you*: I have wiped away the sin you have committed, so obey what I have commanded that you may receive what I have promised.' (Saint Augustine)[25]

5. Monday (alternative Gospel)

> *I am the light of the world. Whoever follows me will never walk in darkness, but will have the light of life.*[26]

Notice how he has called you away from looking with the eyes of the flesh to look with the eyes of your heart. It is not enough to say; *whoever follows me will never walk in darkness but will have the light*, but he added *of life*, like the psalm which says *with you is the fountain of life: in your light we see light*.[27] Notice how these words from the Gospel and the psalm agree, since the psalm speaks of light and of the fountain of life, while the Lord speaks of *the light of life*. When we

speak about material things, light is one thing and a fountain another: our mouths seek a fountain when we are
thirsty and our eyes seek the light when we are in darkness,
and if it happens that we feel thirsty at night, we kindle a
light to show us the way to the fountain. It is not so with
God, with whom light and fountain are the same: he shines
on you that you may see, and flows for you that you may
drink.

You can see, brethren, if you look inwards, what kind of
light it is of which the Lord says *whoever follows me will never
walk in darkness*. If you follow the light of the sun in the sky,
let us see if you do not walk in darkness. It rises in the East
and comes towards you, making its way westwards. Perhaps you have a journey to make towards the East: if you do
not go in the opposite direction from the sun, but follow it,
you will certainly be lost, mistaking West for East. If you follow it on dry land you will be lost, and if a sailor follows it
on the sea, he too will be lost. Suppose you think you should
follow the sun, and you follow it in a westerly direction:
when it sets, we shall see whether or not you walk in darkness. Notice that, although you do not wish to desert it, it
will desert you, bringing the day to a close in accordance
with its duties. But our Lord Jesus Christ, even when his
glory was veiled by the cloud of our flesh, held all things in
the power of his wisdom. Provided you do not fall away
from him, he will never fall below the horizon for you.

He expressed his promise in the future tense, not saying
'has' but *will have the light of life*. But he does not says 'whoever will follow me', but *whoever follows me*. Such a person
follows now, and *will have* later: now he follows by faith, later
he will have by sight since, as the Apostle says, *while we are
at home in the body we are away from the Lord – for we walk by
faith, not by sight*.[28] When shall we walk by sight? When we
have the light of life, when we come to that vision, when this
night shall have passed away. We shall rejoice in the truth
when we see face to face, since that too is promised us. Who

would dare to hope for what God has not deigned to promise or to give? The Apostle says *Now I know only in part, as in a mirror, dimly: then I will see face to face,*[29] and the Apostle John says in his Epistle *Beloved, we are God's children now; what we will be has not yet been revealed. What we do know is this: when he is revealed, we will be like him, for we will see him as he is.*[30] (Saint Augustine)[31]

6. Tuesday

O Lord our God, what is the meaning of those words of yours *unless you believe that I am*?[32] What is there that you have not made? Is the sky not your work, or the earth, or everything that is in earth and heaven? Is not man himself, to whom you speak these words, your own creation? And the messengers whom you send?[33] If all these are your own creation, why is it that you have kept being itself as your own possession, giving it to nothing and nobody else, so that you alone ARE? When I hear I AM WHO AM,[34] does that mean that other things are not? And what of *unless you believe that I am*? Those who heard him – was it not true that they WERE? Even though they were sinners, they were human. Then what must I do? Let him tell me in my heart, deep within me, what BEING is; may my inner self hear and my mind truly grasp what BEING is. True BEING is without change. Every thing, of whatever kind, <> however excellent it may be, if it is subject to change, cannot truly be said to BE, for there is no true BEING where there is also non-being.

Anything that can change, once it has undergone change, is not what it was before. If it is not what it was before, it has undergone a kind of death, and something has been taken away that was there before and now is there no longer. On the head of an old person with white hair, blackness has died; in the body of a bent and exhausted old person, beauty has died; in the body of a sick person, strength has died; standing still has died in the body of a person walking,

walking has died in the body of a person who is standing still, both walking and standing still have died in the body of a person who is lying down, speech has died on the tongue of a person who is silent. When anything changes and is what it was not, I see life in what it is and death in what it was. So when somebody asks about a dead person 'Where is he?', we reply 'He is no more'.

O Truth, you who truly ARE! In all our actions and movements, in every agitation within creation, I see two times, the past and the future. I look for the present, and I find nothing stable; what I have said is no longer, and what I am about to say is not yet; what I have done is no longer, and what I am about to do is not yet: the life I have lived is no longer, and the life that lies before me is not yet. In every movement of things I find a past and a future. In the Truth that endures I find no past, no future, but only an unchanging present, such as does not exist in creatures.

Think of the changes in things, and you will find past and future; think of God, and you will find present, with no place for past or future. So in order to find true BEING, you must rise above time. But who can rise above it by his own power? Let the one who said to his Father, *I desire that those also,... may be with me where I am,*[35] raise us there. It seems to me that the Lord Jesus Christ was promising that we would not die in our sins when he said *unless you believe that I am,* for these words seem to me to mean nothing other than *you will die in your sins unless you believe that I am*[36] GOD. Thanks be to God that he said unless you believe, not 'unless you understand', for who could understand this? But perhaps, since I have been bold enough to speak and you are looking as if you have understood, you have grasped something of this inexpressible mystery? If you have not grasped it, faith sets you free. That is why the Lord did not say 'unless you understand that I am' but he spoke of what was within their power: *you will die in your sins unless you believe that I am.* (Saint Augustine)[37]

7. Wednesday

> *Then Jesus said to the Jews who had believed in him, 'If you*
> *continue in my word, you are truly my disciples; and you*
> *will know the truth, and the truth will make you free.'*[38]

What does he promise to those who believe, brothers and
sisters? *And you will know the truth.* What can this mean? Did
they not know the truth when the Lord spoke to them? And
if they did not know it, how did they believe? They did not
believe because they knew, but they believed in order that
they might know. We believe in order to know: we do not
know in order to believe. For what we are to know is *what no*
eye has seen, nor ear heard, nor the human heart conceived.[39] For
what is faith but believing what you cannot see? Faith, then,
is believing what you do not see, and truth is seeing what
you have believed, as he himself says somewhere.[40] That is
why, in order to establish the faith, the Lord first walked on
the earth. He was a man, he became humble, he was seen by
everybody, but not recognised by everybody; by many he
was rejected, he was killed by the crowd, he was mourned
by only a few, and even by those who mourned him he was
not yet recognised for what he was. All this was the beginning, the outline of the faith and of the structure that was to
be. The Lord knew this when he said somewhere *They who*
have my commandments and keep them are those who love me;
and those who love me will be loved by my Father, and I will love
them and reveal myself to them.[41] Those who heard him could
see him already, and yet he promised that, if they loved him,
they would see him.

Similarly, here he says *you will know the truth.* What does
this mean? Is what you have said not the truth? It is, but it is
still a truth that is believed, not yet a truth that is seen. If we
remain in what we believe, we shall come to that which we
shall see. So the holy evangelist John in his letter says
Beloved, we are God's children now; what we will be has not yet

been revealed.[42] We are now, and there is something that we shall become. What can we be that is more than we are already? Listen: *What we do know is this: when he is revealed, we will be like him,* why? *For we will see him as he is.*[43] This is a wonderful promise, but it is the reward of faith. If you seek the reward, let the deed precede it. If you believe, ask for the reward of faith, but if you do not, what right have you to ask for the reward of faith? So *If you continue in my word, you will be truly my disciples,*[44] to contemplate the truth as it really is, not through the sound of words but through brilliant light when he satisfies our hunger, as the Psalm says, *Let the light of your face shine on us, O Lord!.*[45] We are God's coinage, but we are like coins who have been lost and are far from the treasury where they belong. The mark that was imprinted on us has been worn away in our wanderings. He is coming to restore us, for he it was who made us. He comes to claim his coin, as the emperor claims his, which is why he says *Give to the emperor the things that are the emperor's, and to God the things that are God's,*[46] that is, coins to the emperor, and to God your very selves. Then the truth will be seen in us. (Saint Augustine)[47]

8. Thursday

'*Very truly, I tell you, whoever keeps my word will never see death.*'[48]

The Lord spoke these words to people who were destined to die, just as he himself was, since *to GOD, the Lord, belongs the departure of death,*[49] as the Psalm says. In that case, what does he mean by saying *whoever keeps my word will never see death*? The Lord must have had in view another death from which he came to set us free, the second death, the eternal death, the death of hell, of damnation with the devil and his angels. That is the true death, for the other death is nothing more than a journey. It is departure from the body, the laying down of a heavy load, but only if a person is not carrying a heavier burden, one that will drag him down into hell. That was the death the Lord was speaking of when he said *whoever keeps my word will never see death.* There is no need for us to be afraid of the first death, but we should fear the second. <>

You were born a human being, and you will die. Where can you go to escape death? What will you do to ensure that you do not die? The Lord consented to a voluntary death to console those whose death is unavoidable. When you look on the dead Christ, do you consider yourself above death? You are going to die: you have no way of avoiding it. It may be today, it may be tomorrow, but it will come, the debt must be paid. So what are people doing being afraid, running away, hiding themselves to avoid being found by the enemy? Are they trying to escape death? No, only delaying their death for a short time. Their debt is not cancelled, but they ask for the date of payment to be put off. However long it is put off, eventually the day will come.

Let us rather fear that death which the three young men were afraid of when they said *our God whom we serve is able to deliver us from the furnace of blazing fire,... but if he does not...*[50] they were afraid of the death with which the Lord is threatening us here in the Gospel, since they were saying '... but if he does not wish to deliver us openly, he is able to crown us secretly'. That is why the Lord, who was to become the chief of martyrs and to make others martyrs, said *do not fear those who kill the body, and after that can do nothing more.*[51] Why is it that they *can do nothing more*? They can kill a body and then throw it out to be ripped apart by animals and torn up by birds, and still there remain things for them to do in their savagery. But to whom are they doing these things? To one who has gone away. The body is there, but it has no feeling left. The dwelling lies on the ground, but the householder has gone away. Once that has happened, they can do nothing more, since they can do nothing to a person who has no feeling left. *Rather fear him who can destroy both soul and body in hell.*[52] That was the death of which he was speaking when he said *whoever keeps my word will never see death.* So, brothers and sisters, let us keep his words in faith, so that we may come to see him on that day when we shall receive total freedom. (Saint Augustine)[53]

9. Friday

> *The Jews took up stones again to stone him. Jesus replied, 'I have shown you many good works from the Father. For which of these are you going to stone me?' The Jews answered, 'It is not for a good work that we are going to stone you, but for blasphemy, because you, though only a human being, are making yourself God.'*[54]

They said this because he had said I and the Father are one.[55] You see, the Jews understood what Arians[56] do not understand. They were angry because they realised that I and the Father are one can only be said when there is equality between Father and Son.

See how the Lord replied to these slow-witted people. He saw that they could not endure the splendour of the truth, so he concealed it in the way in which he spoke: Is it not written in your law, 'I said, you are gods'?[57] If God's word to man calls men gods, how can it be that the Word of God himself, who is with God, is not God? If God's words make men gods, if they become divine by sharing in the divine life, how can it be that the source of their sharing is not God? If those who receive light are gods, how can the light that enlightens them not be God? You draw near to the light and are enlightened and counted among the children of God; if you withdraw from the light you grow dark and are counted among those who are in darkness; but that light does not draw near to itself because it does not withdraw from itself. So if God's word makes you gods, how can the Word of God not be God? So the Father has sanctified his Son and sent

him into the world.[58] Somebody may say, 'if the Father consecrated him, was there then a time when he was not holy?'
He consecrated him in the same way as he begot him, for in
begetting him he gave him his holiness: he begot him holy. If
only something that is not already holy can be made holy,
how is it that we say to God the Father Hallowed be thy
name?

The Son does not say the Father is in me and *I am in the
Father*[59] as human beings might say it. If our thoughts are
good we are in God, and if we live good lives God is in us;
we, the faithful who share in his grace and are enlightened
by him, are in him and he is in us. But with the only-begotten Son it is different: he is in the Father and the Father in
him as equals. We can sometimes say 'God is in us and we
are in God', but can we ever say 'I and God are one'? You
are in God because God holds you, God is in you because
you have become a temple of God, <> but can you say 'whoever sees me sees God' like the only Son who says *He who
has seen me has seen the Father*[60] and *The Father and I are one*?[61]
Notice that what belongs to the Lord by right is given to the
servant as a gift. It is by right that the Lord is equal with the
Father; it is by gift that the servant shares in the life of the
Saviour. (Saint Augustine)[62]

10. Saturday

Now the Passover of the Jews was near.[63]

The Jews wanted to make that feast bloody with the blood of
the Lord. They had a plan to kill Jesus, and he who had
come from heaven to suffer wanted to come near to the
place of his suffering, for the hour of his passion was near.
*And many went up from the country to Jerusalem before the
Passover to purify themselves.*[64] The Jews did this according to
the commandment of the Lord which had been given in the
law through holy Moses that on the feast of the Passover

they should all come together from everywhere and be sanctified by the celebration of that day. But that celebration was *a shadow of what was to come.*[65] What is that? A prophecy of the Christ who was to come, who was to suffer for us on that day, that the shadow might pass away and the light come, that signs might pass away and the truth remain. So the Jews had the Passover in shadow, and we have it in the light. What point was there in the Lord's commanding them to kill a sheep during that feast-day unless he was the one of whom it was said in prophecy that he was *like a lamb that is led to the slaughter?*[66] The doorposts of the Jews were marked with the blood of a slaughtered lamb, and our foreheads are marked with the blood of Christ.[67] That mark, because it had a meaning, is said to ward off the destroyer from the houses that are marked with it: the mark of Christ wards off the destroyer from us if our heart makes the Saviour welcome.

Why have I said this? Because many have the sign on their doorposts, but there is nobody in the house: they carry the sign of Christ easily on their foreheads but do not welcome the word of Christ in their hearts. So, brethren, I repeat what I have said, that the sign of Christ drives the destroyer away from us provided that Christ dwells in our hearts.[68] I have said these things in case anybody is wondering what these Jewish festivals mean for him. The Lord came like a victim to the sacrifice that we might have the true Passover when we celebrate his suffering like the sacrifice of a sheep. *They were looking for Jesus,*[69] but in a bad way. Blessed are those who look for Jesus in a good way. They were not looking for Jesus in order that either they or we might have him, but we received him when he went away from them. <> So let us look for Christ in order that we may have him and hold on to him, not in order that we may kill him, for they were looking for him in order to hold him and then to lose him quickly. (Saint Augustine)[70]

NOTES

1. John 11:14-15
2. *Commentary on John* 49, 2-3; *PL* 35, 1747-1748
3. John 12:24-25
4. John 12:26
5. John 12:27-28
6. Matt 26:38-39
7. Matt 26:39
8. John 12:28
9. John 21:18
10. John 21:19
11. *Commentary on John* 52, 2-3; *PL* 35, 1769-1770
12. John 8:3-6
13. Luke 19:10
14. John 8:7
15. Because fruit grows from the earth, not from stones.
16. 1 Cor 2:11
17. John 8:9
18. John 8:8
19. *Commentary on John* 33, 4-5; *PL* 35, 1648-1650
20. John 8:7
21. John 8:10
22. John 8:11
23. Ps 25:8
24. cf. Ezek 18:21-22; 33:14-15
25. *Commentary on John* 33, 6-8; *PL* 35, 1650-1651
26. John 8:12
27. Ps 36:9
28. 2 Cor 5:6-7
29. cf. 1 Cor 13:12
30. 1 John 3:2
31. *Commentary on John* 34, 5-9; *PL* 35, 1654-1656
32. John 8:24
33. i.e. the angels

34. Ex 3:14
35. John 17:24
36. John 8:24
37. *Commentary on John* 38, 10; *PL* 35, 1679-1681
38. John 8:31-32
39. 1 Cor 2:9
40. Cf. *Jesus said to her, 'Did I not tell you that if you believed, you would see the glory of God?'* (John 11:40).
41. John 14:21
42. 1 John 3:2
43. 1 John 3:2
44. John 8:31
45. Ps 4:6
46. Matt 22:21
47. *Commentary on John* 40, 9; *PL* 35, 1690-1691
48. John 8:51
49. Ps 68:20
50. Dan 3:17-18
51. Luke 12:4
52. Matt 10:28
53. *Commentary on John* 43, 11-12; *PL* 35, 1710-1711
54. John 10:31-33
55. John 10:30
56. Those who deny that God the Son is equal to God the Father.
57. Ps 81:6
58. John 10:36
59. John 10:38
60. John 14:9
61. John 10:30
62. *Commentary on John* 48, 8-12; *PL* 35, 1744-1746
63. John 11:55
64. John 11:55
65. Col 2:17
66. Is 53:7
67. There was a custom in the early church of communicants

moistening their hands with the Blood of Christ while it was still on their lips, and touching with it other parts of the body, including the forehead. Cf. Cyril of Jerusalem, *Mystagogical Catechesis* 5, 22; *PG* 33, 1125.

68. cf. Eph 3:17
69. John 11:56
70. *Commentary on John* 50, 1-3; *PL* 35, 1758-1759

7

HOLY WEEK

1. Sunday Year A: Gospel for the Procession

When they had come near Jerusalem and had reached Beth-phage, at the Mount of Olives, Jesus sent two disciples, saying to them, 'Go into the village ahead of you, and immediately you will find a donkey tied, and a colt with her; untie them and bring them to me'.[1]

Not only did Jesus fulfil the prophecies and plant true doctrine among us, but by what he did he taught us how to live, setting a standard for what we should do and setting our lives on the right path.

For this reason, when the time came for him to be born, he did not look for a splendid house or a wealthy and distinguished mother, but a poor woman who had a carpenter for a fiancé, and he was born in a shed and laid in a manger. When he chose his followers, he did not choose good orators or clever people, or wealthy and noble people, but poor men born from poor parents, who were altogether undistinguished. When he prepared a meal, at one time he set barley loaves on the table, and at another he told his disciples to go shopping in the market for what they needed. When he made his bed, he made it of grass; for his clothing he chose cheap materials, no different from what anybody else would wear.

He had no house of his own. When he needed to travel from one place to another, he did so on foot, and he grew weary from travelling. When he sat down, he did not demand a throne or a cushion, but sat on the ground, sometimes on a mountain and once by a well. Not only did he sit

103

by a well, but he sat there alone, talking to a Samaritan woman. When he was moved to tears, he was moderate in his grief. Everywhere, as I have said, he set standards and limits to show that we should go so far and no further. For the same reason now, since some people need animals to carry them because of weakness, he sets a standard, showing that we should not use horses or mules in harness for our transport, but an ass and nothing superior, and that in everything we should restrict ourselves to what we need. (Saint John Chrysostom)[2]

2. Sunday Year A: The Passion

From noon on, darkness came over the whole land until three in the afternoon.[3]

This is the sign Jesus had promised earlier to those who asked for a sign, saying *An evil and adulterous generation asks for a sign, but no sign will be given to it except the sign of the prophet Jonah,*[4] by which he meant his Cross, his death, his burial and his resurrection. He also spoke of the power of the Cross in another way when he said *When you have lifted up the Son of Man, then you will realise that I am he.*[5] What he means is this: 'When you crucify me and think that you have overcome me, then above all you shall know my power'.

This is because after the Crucifixion the city of Jerusalem was destroyed, the Jewish state came to an end, their politics and their freedom were no more, while the preaching of the Gospel flourished, and the Word reached to the ends of the world. The earth and the sea, the inhabited parts of the world and the desert everywhere proclaim his power. These are the things he is speaking of, and they came about at the time of his Crucifixion. It was much more wonderful that these things happened when he was nailed to the Cross than if he had been walking the earth. <>

Many women were also there, looking on from a distance; they had followed Jesus from Galilee and had provided for him. Among them were Mary Magdalene, and Mary the mother of James and Joseph, and the mother of the sons of Zebedee.[6] The women, who feel the greatest sympathy with him and are most touched with grief for him, witness these things. See how great is their care for him. They had followed him and ministered to him, and remained with him in his hour of peril. So they saw everything, how he cried out, how he breathed out his spirit, how the rocks were split and everything else.

These are the first to see Jesus: the sex that is most blamed is the first to enjoy the sight of his blessings, and shows more manly courage than anybody else. The disciples fled, but they remained. <>

Mary Magdalene and the other Mary were there, sitting opposite the tomb.[7] Why did they wait there? As yet they did not know any of the great and lofty truths about him. They brought ointments and waited patiently beside the tomb in case the fury of the Jews might abate so that they could go and gather round him. Do you see the courage of these women? Do you see their tender care? Do you see their generosity in giving, a generosity that even risks death?

Men, let us imitate the women: let us not forsake Jesus in temptations. They spent so much on him even after his death, and exposed their own lives to danger. But we do not feed him when he is hungry or clothe him when he is naked: when we see him begging we hurry past him. If you could see that it is he, each of you would give away all his possessions. But it is he, even now, for he himself has said *I am he.*[8] So why do you not give everything? You can hear him speaking now 'you do it to me',[9] and it makes no difference whether you give to him or to somebody else. (Saint John Chrysostom)[10]

3. Sunday Year B: Gospel for the Procession

Blessed is the coming kingdom of our ancestor David! Hosanna in the highest heaven![11]

We read in the Gospel of John that the crowds who had been fed with the five loaves and the two fish wanted to capture Jesus and make him king, but that he withdrew to the mountain to pray so that they could not do this.[12] But now that he comes to Jerusalem to suffer, he does not flee those who make him a king, leading him to the royal city in a triumphal procession with songs fit for a king and the Son of God; he does not silence the voices of those who sing that the kingdom of the patriarch David will be renewed in him and the blessings of former times restored. So why does he now gladly embrace what he formerly fled and refused, and now that he is about to leave the world through the suffering of the Cross, why does he not decline the kingdom that he would not accept while he was still living in the world, if not to teach us openly that he is the king, not of a temporal and earthly kingdom, but of an eternal one in heaven? To this kingdom he was to come through the shame of his death, the glory of his resurrection and the triumph of his ascension. <> Note how the song of the crowd that acclaims the Lord agrees with the words of Gabriel when he brought good news to his virgin mother, saying *he will be great, and will be called the Son of the Most High, and the Lord God will give to him the throne of his ancestor David. He will reign over the house of Jacob forever*.[13] The Lord received the throne or kingdom of David so that by words, deeds, gifts and promises worthy of so great *a mediator between God and humankind*[14] he might call to the immortal kingdom of heaven and bring to the vision of God the Father that nation which David once ruled by his power, instructed by his example of justice and aroused by his spiritual songs[15] to faith and love towards its Creator. The song of the crowd ends *Hosanna*, that is, salvation, *in the highest heaven*! This shows clearly that the coming of Christ was salvation not only for humankind, but for the whole universe, joining earth to heaven so that to him every knee should bend, in heaven and on earth and under the earth.[16] (Saint Bede)[17]

4. Sunday Year B: The Passion

And they crucified him, and divided his clothes among them, casting lots to decide what each should take.[18]

The evangelist John explains this more fully: they divided the rest of his clothing into four parts, one for each soldier, but they cast lots for his tunic since it was seamless, woven in one piece from the top.

The division of the Lord's clothes into four signifies the Church which is divided into four equal parts, that is, extended harmoniously, throughout all the four parts of the world. The tunic for which lots were cast signifies the unity of these four parts of the Church, which are held together by the bond of charity. If charity is, as the Apostle says, a higher way, higher than knowledge and above all the commandments, then the garment by which it is signified is rightly said to be woven from the top. As for the lots cast by all the soldiers, they mean nothing other than the grace of God which comes to all who abide in unity: when the lots are cast, no account is taken of a person's dignity or merits, but all depends on God's grace. Since, as the Apostle says, *our old self was crucified with him so that the body of sin might be destroyed, and we might no longer be enslaved to sin,*[19] as long as our deeds are such as to destroy the body of sin, and as long as *our outer nature is wasting away* so that *our inner nature* may be *renewed from day to day,*[20] it is the time of the Cross. These are good works, but laborious ones, and their reward is rest. But Saint Paul says *rejoice in hope*[21] to help us work gladly for the rest that awaits us. This gladness is signified by the breadth of the horizontal beam of the Cross where the hands are fixed, since hands are a symbol of work and breadth a symbol of the joy of the workman, since narrowness is a result of sadness. The upper part of the Cross, where the head is, signifies the expectation of the retribution that will come from the high justice of God, who *will repay everyone according to their deeds:*[22] to some, who lead good and patient lives and seek eternal life, he will give glory, honour and incorruption. And the longest part of the Cross, along which the whole body is stretched, signifies patience, since patient people are called 'long-suffering'. As for the lowest part, which is fixed in the earth, this signifies the secrets of God's mysterious design. You will notice, I am sure, that this explanation of the Cross explains the words of the Apostle *you are being rooted and grounded in love... that you may have the power to comprehend, with all the saints, what is the breadth and length and height and depth.*[23]

The inscription of the charge against him read, 'The King of the Jews'.[24] This title shows that even by killing him they could not escape having him as king who will *repay* them *according to their deeds* with the splendour of his supreme power made visible. So in the Psalm we sing, *I have set my king on Zion, my holy hill*.[25] As he offered to the Father on the altar of the Cross the supreme sacrifice of his own flesh, it was suitable that he should also proclaim his royal dignity by means of this inscription, since he is both king and priest, so as to teach all who are willing to read, that is, to hear and to believe, that by his suffering on the Cross he did not lose his kingly power, but rather confirmed and strengthened it. (Saint Bede)[26]

5. Sunday Year C: Gospel for the Procession

When he had come near Bethphage and Bethany, at the place called the Mount of Olives, he sent two of the disciples, saying, 'Go into the village ahead of you, and as you enter it you will find tied there a colt that has never been ridden. Untie it and bring it here.'... Then they brought it to Jesus; and after throwing their cloaks on the colt, they set Jesus on it.[27]

The Lord of the world was carried on a colt's back, not because this would make a pleasing spectacle, but in order to take his seat secretly within us like a mystic rider, guiding with his divine power the footsteps of our minds and bridling

our fleshly desires. <> Learn from God's friends how to carry
Christ, for he first carried you, a shepherd bringing back a
wandering sheep: learn spiritually to carry him, to be under
Christ, in order that you may be above the world. It is not
everybody who can easily carry Christ, but only the person
who can say *I am utterly spent and crushed; I groan because of the
tumult of my heart.*[28] If you wish to walk steadily, keep your
footsteps clean by walking on the garments of the saints – for
in the holy scriptures 'garments' is often used to mean
'virtues'.[29] Take care that your feet do not become dirty as you
walk; take care that your steps do not wander from the path
prepared for you by those who have gone before. That you
may walk without stumbling, the Lord's disciples have
stripped themselves of the garments of their own bodies and
have prepared your path through adversity by their own
martyrdom. <>

So do not despise this colt, for just as there are ravenous
wolves who come in sheep's clothing, so beneath the appearance of an animal lies the hidden heart of man, for within the
outward casing of the body, which we have in common with
the beasts, lives a mind filled with God. And do not despise
the donkey, for a donkey once saw an angel of God whom no
man could see.[30] She saw him and revealed his presence and
spoke, as a sign that later, when the great Angel of God came,
the gentiles,[31] who had previously been like donkeys, would
begin to speak. <> So the crowd recognises Jesus as God, hails
him as King, and repeats the words of the Prophet *Hosanna to
the son of David!*,[32] proclaiming that the long-awaited
redeemer of the house of David has come, a son of David
after the flesh – and this is the crowd that in a very short time
is to crucify him. (Saint Ambrose)[33]

6. Sunday Year C: The Passion

*The soldiers also mocked him, coming up and offering him
sour wine.*[34]

To bring all things to completion, it is fitting that he drinks the corruption of purity, that everything that has been spoiled may be fixed to the cross. So he drinks sour wine, but not wine mixed with gall,[35] not because of the gall, but because he refused bitterness mixed with wine. He certainly took on the bitterness of our life when he lived among us in the body, and he himself says *they gave me gall for food, and for my thirst they gave me vinegar to drink*.[36] But bitterness was not to be mixed with purity, to show that there would be no bitterness in the everlasting life of the resurrection, and that this everlasting life, which had turned sour in human vessels, has been renewed in Christ. So he drinks sour wine, that is, the corruption of immortality which came about through Adam is destroyed, that it may have no power over the human body. Let us too pour on to Christ the sins we have committed through carelessness in mind and body, let us pour them over him through baptism that we may be crucified in Christ, let us pour them over him through penance, that he may in his turn pour upon us the incorrupt purity of heavenly wine and blood.

Then, when he had drunk the sour wine, he said *all things are fulfilled*,[37] because the mystery of his taking on mortality was fulfilled, and now that all sin had been overcome, only the joy of immortality remained.

And so he says *Lord, into your hands I commend my spirit*.[38] He is rightly said to 'commend' his spirit, since he does not give it away, for what is commended is not lost. The Spirit is a guarantee of good things to come,[39] a good treasure, which leads Saint Paul to say *O Timothy, guard the good treasure entrusted to you.* Jesus commends his spirit to the Father, and so he says *for you will not leave my soul in hell*.[40] But notice a great mystery. Now, at the same time as he is commending his spirit into the hands of the Father, he is sitting in the bosom of the Father, for nobody else can contain the whole Christ. Moreover, he says *I am in the Father and the Father is in me*,[41] and so it is to the Father that he commends his spirit.

But since he is on high, he sheds light into hell as well, that the entire universe may be redeemed. *Christ is all and in all*,[42] although Christ works in each person individually. The flesh dies that it may rise again, the spirit is commended to the Father that the realms above may also be released from the bondage of sin and that there may be peace in heaven, to be followed by peace on earth.

And having said this, he gave up his spirit.[43] The evangelist rightly says 'gave up', since he did not lose his spirit unwillingly. Matthew says *he set loose his spirit*,[44] for we set things loose willingly, whereas we lose them against our will. That is why Matthew added *with a loud voice*.[45] In this cry we may hear either Jesus' boast that he has come down even to death for our sins – so that I shall not be ashamed to profess what Christ was not ashamed to proclaim with a loud voice – or a clear sign from God witnessing the separation of Christ's divinity from his body. These are the words: *Jesus cried out with a loud voice, 'My God, my God, look on me! why have you forsaken me?'*[46] The man cried out as he was about to die with the separation of divinity from his body, for since divinity is free of death, there could be no death unless life withdrew, for divinity is life. (Saint Ambrose)[47]

7. Monday

Mary took a pound of costly perfume made of pure nard, anointed Jesus' feet, and wiped them with her hair. The house was filled with the fragrance of the perfume.[48]

Now that we have heard the story, let us seek the mystery that it contains. If you wish to be a faithful soul, whoever you are, join Mary in anointing the feet of the Lord with precious ointment. The ointment was justice, which is why it weighed a pound.[49] It was *costly perfume made of pure nard*: the Latin for 'pure' is *pisticus*, <> a name very suitable for the mystery we are considering, since *pistis* in Greek means 'faith'. You want to do deeds of justice: *The just person lives by faith*.[50] Anoint the feet of Jesus: follow in the Lord's footsteps by living a good life. Wipe his feet with your hair: if you have superfluous possessions, give them to the poor and you will have wiped the feet of the Lord, for the hair seems superfluous to the body. There is something for you to do with your excess possessions: to you they are superfluous, but they are necessary for the feet of the Lord. Perhaps the feet of the Lord on earth are in need, since it is of his members that he will say at the end *when you did it to the least of my members, you did it to me*.[51] That is, 'you gave away what was superfluous to you, but you did service and honour to my feet '.

The house was filled with the fragrance of the perfume:[52] that means that the world was filled with her good name, for a good name is a sweet perfume. Those who are called Christians and live evil lives do injury to Christ, and Scripture says that because of them *the name of God is blasphemed*.[53] If the name of the Lord is blasphemed because of people like that, then his name is praised because of the virtuous. Listen to the Apostle: *we are the aroma of Christ... in every place*.[54] And the Song of Songs says *your name is perfume poured out*.[55] <>

You always have the poor with you, but you do not always have me:[56] Jesus was speaking of the presence of his body. According to his majesty, his providence, his invisible and indescribable grace, these words of his are true: *I am with you always, to the end of the age*,[57] but according to the flesh that the Word assumed, according to that which was born of the Virgin, captured by the Jews, fixed to the wood of the Cross, taken down, wrapped in linen, hidden in a tomb and revealed in the resurrection, that *you do not always have*. Why? Because he lived in his bodily presence with the disciples for forty days and, as their eyes followed him but they did not go with him, he ascended into heaven and he is not here. He is there, at the right hand of the Father, and he is here, because the presence of his majesty has not gone away.

In other words, we always have Christ according to the presence of his majesty, but as for the presence of his flesh he rightly said to his disciples *you do not always have me*. The Church had him with her in the flesh for a few days: now she holds on to him by faith without seeing him with her eyes. (Saint Augustine)[58]

8. Tuesday

What did the Lord say after Judas had gone out to do quickly what he was going to do? What said the Day, when Night had gone out? What said the Redeemer when the Purchaser had gone out? *Now the Son of Man has been glorified*.[59] Why now? Was it because his betrayer had gone out, and those who were to capture and kill him were near? Did he say *Now* he *has been glorified* because the time has come for him to be humiliated further, because he will soon be bound, judged, condemned, mocked, crucified and killed? Is this glorification, or is it not rather humiliation? When he was doing miracles, did not this John say the Spirit had not been given, because Jesus was not yet glorified?[60] Was he not yet glorified when he raised the dead, and is he glorified now, when he will soon be joining the dead? Was he not yet glorified when doing acts of divine power, and is he glorified now that he is about to undergo human suffering? It would be surprising if that was what our divine Master meant to teach us by these words.

We must look more deeply into these words of the Most High, who sometimes reveals himself so that we may find him, and then hides himself again that we may seek him and press forward as it were step by step from one discovery to another. I see in these words a sign of something great that still lies in the future. Judas went out, and Jesus was glorified: the son of perdition went out, and the Son of Man was glorified. The man had gone out on whose account the words *and you are clean, though not all of you*[61] had been said to them. And so when the unclean one went out, all those

113

who were left were clean, and they remained with the one who made them clean. Something similar will take place when this world, conquered by Christ, will pass away, and nobody unclean will remain among Christ's people, when the weeds will have been separated from the grain and *the righteous will shine like the sun in the kingdom of their Father.*[62]

The Lord was looking forward to this and witnessing to a sign of it in the present when Judas went out like the weeds and the Apostles remained like the grain, and he said *Now the Son of Man has been glorified*, as if he were saying 'See how it will be when I am glorified, when none of the wicked will remain and none of the good will be lost'. But he did not say 'Now the glorification of the Son of man has been signified', but *Now the Son of Man has been glorified*, just as Scripture does not say 'the rock signified Christ', but *the rock was Christ*, nor does it say 'the good seed signified the children of the kingdom' or 'the weeds signified the children of the evil one', but *the good seed are the children of the kingdom; the weeds are the children of the evil one.*[63] So just as Scripture is accustomed to speak of signs as if they were the realities they signify, so the Lord said *Now the Son of Man has been glorified* after the evil one had been separated from them and his saints remained with him as a sign of his glorification, when the wicked will be taken away and he will remain in eternity with his saints. (Saint Augustine)[64]

9. Wednesday

When it was evening, he took his place with the twelve.[65]

See the shamelessness of Judas! He too was there and came to share the mysteries and the food, and his guilt is shown at the very table where, even if he had been a wild beast, he would have become tame. For this reason the evangelist tells us that as they ate Christ spoke about his betrayal so as to show the wickedness of the betrayer from the time that he chose for his deed and the fact that they sat together at table. *And while they were eating, he said, 'Truly I tell you, one of you will betray me.'*[66] Before supper he had even washed Judas' feet. And see how he spares the traitor: he did not say 'this man will betray me' but *one of you* so as to give him a chance of repentance by not revealing his identity, and he prefers to alarm all the disciples in the hope of saving this one. 'One of you', he says, 'one of the Twelve who have been everywhere with me, whose feet I have washed, to whom I have promised so much'. And so unbearable sorrow caught hold of that holy brotherhood. <>

But somebody will say, 'If it has been written that he must suffer these things, why is Judas blamed?' Because he did what was written out of wickedness, rather than with the intention of fulfilling the prophecies. Unless you look for the motive of a deed, you will excuse even the devil of his crimes. That would be wrong, for both Judas and the devil deserve infinite punishment, even though the world has been saved. It was not Judas' treachery that caused our salvation but the wisdom of Christ and the great skill by which he turned the wickedness of others to our advantage. 'What then?' someone may say, 'if Judas had not betrayed him, would not somebody else have done so?' What is that to do with the matter? 'If Jesus had to be crucified, it had to happen through somebody like Judas. If everybody had been good, our salvation would have been prevented.' This is not true, for God the wholly wise knew how he would care for us, even had this been so, since his resourcefulness and his wisdom cannot be thwarted. So, lest anybody think that Judas has become a minister of our redemption, he declares the wretchedness of the man. But again, somebody will ask 'if it would have been better for him not to have been born, why did he allow him and all other wicked people to come into the world?' You should blame the wicked because they have become wicked although they had the power not to be so, but instead you are busy with curiosity about the things of God, even though you know that nobody is wicked by necessity. 'But only the good should have been born, and then there would be no need of hell or punishment or vengeance or any trace of sin, and wicked people would either not be born or else vanish immediately.' In reply, I would first remind you of the Apostle's words *But who indeed are you, a human being, to argue with God? Will what is moulded say to the one who moulds it, 'Why have you made me like this?'*[67] But if you still ask for reasons, I would say that good people are more admired for existing among the wicked, since thus their tolerance and wisdom are more apparent, but by speaking as you do you remove their opportunities for exertion and struggle. 'Why then, are others punished in order that these may be seen to be good?' Certainly not: they are punished for their own wickedness, since they did not become wicked because they were born, but because of their own moral laxity, and that is why they are punished. How can they not deserve punishment, since they have such great teachers to instruct them in virtue and have learned nothing from them? Just as the noble and the good deserve double honour both because they have become virtuous and also because they have lived among sinners, so also the wicked deserve double punishment both for having become wicked when they could have become good, and also for having learned nothing from the virtuous. (Saint John Chrysostom)[68]

NOTES

1. Matt 21:2
2. *Commentary on Matthew* 66, 2; *PG* 58, 628
3. Matt 27:45
4. Matt 12:39
5. John 8:28
6. Matt 27:55-56
7. Matt 27:61

8. John 8:24
9. cf. Matt 25:40
10. *Commentary on Matthew* 88, 1-3; *PG* 58, 775-778
11. Mark 11:10
12. John 6:15
13. Luke 1:32-33
14. 1 Tim 2:5
15. Bede, in continuity with patristic tradition, regarded King David as the author of all the Psalms.
16. Phil 2:10
17. *Commentary on Mark* 3, 11; *PL* 92, 242-243
18. Mark 15:24
19. Rom 6:6
20. 2 Cor 4:16
21. Rom 12:12
22. Matt 16:27
23. Eph 3:17-18
24. Mark 15:26
25. Ps 2:6
26. *Commentary on Mark* 4, 15; *PL* 92, 287-288
27. Luke 19:29-30;35
28. Ps 38:9
29. cf. Job 29:14; 1 Pet 5:5
30. Num 22:23
31. The Jews are often represented by an ox and the Gentiles by an ass beside the manger at Bethlehem in depictions of Christ's nativity.
32. Matt 21:15
33. *Commentary on Luke* 9, 9-15; *PL* 15, 1887-1888
34. Luke 23:36
35. Matt 27:34
36. Ps 69:21
37. cf. John 19:30
38. Ps 31:6; cf. Luke 23:46
39. cf. 2 Cor 1:22; 5:5
40. Ps 16:10

41. John 14:11
42. Col 3:11
43. Luke 23:46
44. Matt 27:50
45. Matt 27:46;50
46. cf. Matt 27:46; Ps 22:1
47. *Commentary on Luke* 10, 124-127; *PL* 15, 1927-1929
48. John 12:3
49. The Latin word *libra* means both 'a pound weight' and 'a pair of scales'; scales were and are a well-known symbol of justice.
50. Rom 1:17
51. Matt 25:40
52. John 12:3
53. Rom 2:24
54. cf. 2 Cor 2:14-15
55. Songs 1:2
56. John 12:8
57. Matt 28:20
58. *Commentary on John* 50, 6-13; *PL* 35, 1760-1763
59. John 13:31
60. John 7:39
61. John 13:10
62. Matt 13:40-43
63. Matt 13:38
64. *Commentary on John* 63, 2; *PL* 35, 1804-1805
65. Matt 26:20
66. Matt 26:21
67. Rom 9:20
68. *Commentary on Matthew* 81, 1-3; *PG* 58, 731-733

8

THE PASCHAL TRIDUUM

1. Maundy Thursday

Now before the Paschal festival, Jesus knew that his hour had come to depart from this world and go to the Father. Having loved his own who were in the world he loved them to the end.[1]

Brethren, our word *Pasch*[2] comes not from Greek, as some people think, but from Hebrew, but very suitably there is a certain similarity between the two languages in their use of this word. In Greek 'to suffer' is *paschein*, so that some people think Pasch means 'suffering'. But in Hebrew, the language to which it belongs, Pasch means 'crossing over', which is why the people of God celebrated the Paschal feast for the first time when they had crossed over the Red Sea in their flight from Egypt. But now that prophetic sign of the future has been fulfilled in truth, since Christ was *led like a lamb to the slaughter*,[3] and our doorposts are smeared with his blood,[4] that is, our foreheads are marked with the sign of his Cross, and we are freed from the destruction of this world as if from captivity or death in Egypt, and we cross over in utmost safety when we pass from the devil to Christ, from this unstable world to his kingdom, built as it is on the most solid of foundations. We pass over to the God who endures, so that we may not pass away with this passing world.

The Apostle praises God for this grace which he has bestowed on us, saying *He has rescued us from the power of darkness and transferred us into the kingdom of his beloved Son.*[5] So the evangelist is giving an interpretation of this word

Pasch, which means 'pass over', when he says *before the Paschal festival Jesus knew that his hour had come to depart from this world and go to the Father*. There is his *Pasch*, there is his passing over, <> *from this world . . . to the Father*. Thus in the Head hope is given to his members that they will doubtless follow him where he has passed over. So what of unbelievers, who are not joined to this Head and to his Body? Clearly, they do pass over, but it is one thing to pass over from the world, and another to pass over with the world: one way leads to the Father, the other to the Enemy. The Egyptians passed over, but not through the sea to the kingdom: they passed over in the sea to death.

Having loved his own who were in the world he loved them to the end. This was so that by means of his love they too might pass from this world to their Head, who had departed from it. What does *to the end* mean? Surely it means 'to Christ', for the Apostle says *Christ is the end of the law so that there may be righteousness for everyone who believes*.[6] This end is perfection, not death, an end to which we travel, not an end where we perish. That is how we must understand *Christ our Pasch has been sacrificed for us*:[7] he is our end; our passing over is to him. (Saint Augustine)[8]

2. Good Friday

Jesus knew that all was now finished.[9]

Which of us is able to control our actions as well as this man controlled his sufferings? But this man is the *mediator between God and man*,[10] the man of whom the prophetic words were written *he is a man, and who will recognise him*?[11] because the men through whom these things were done did not recognise that this man was God. Visibly he was man; invisibly he was God: the visible one suffered all these things while the invisible one, the same Person, determined what was to take place. For this reason he knew that all that was necessary was finished <> Then, when everything he had been waiting for had happened, and nothing remained to be done before his death, since he had power over his life, *to lay it down and . . . to take it up again,*[12] *he bowed his head and gave up his spirit.*[13] Which of us is able to fall asleep when we will like Jesus, who died when he willed? Which of us can take off our clothes when we will like him who cast aside the garment of his flesh when he willed? Which of us can depart when we will like him who died when he willed? If this is the power he showed in death, what should we hope or fear from the power he will show when he comes in judgment! <>

One of the soldiers opened his side with a spear, and at once blood and water came out.[14] The evangelist was careful to say, not that the soldier 'struck' Jesus' side or 'wounded' it or anything else, but that he opened it in order that the door of life might be unlocked in that place from which the sacraments of the Church flowed out, without which nobody can enter that life which is truly life. That blood was shed for the remission of sins, that water is mingled in the cup of salvation and both cleanses us and slakes our thirst. This was prefigured by the order that was given to Noah, that he was to put the door in the side of the ark,[15] as an entrance for the animals who were to survive the flood, who were a sign of the Church to come. For the same reason the first woman was made from the side of the man as he slept,[16] and she was called the life and mother of all the living.[17] This was a sign of a great good before the great evil of sin. Jesus, the second Adam, bowed his head in sleep on the Cross that a bride might be made for him from the flood that poured from his side. O death through which the dead rise to life! What is more pure than that blood? What is more healthy than that wound?

Now there was a garden in the place where he was crucified. and in the garden there was a new tomb in which no one had ever been laid.[18] Just as in the womb of the virgin Mary nobody was conceived before him or after him, so nobody was buried before him or after him in this tomb. (Saint Augustine)[19]

3. The Paschal Vigil Year A

And suddenly there was a great earthquake: for an angel of the Lord, descending from heaven came and rolled back the stone and sat on it. His appearance was like lightning, and his clothing white as snow. For fear of him the guards shook and became like dead men. But the angel said to the women 'Do not be afraid; I know that you are looking for Jesus who was crucified'.[20]

After the resurrection came the Angel. Why did he come and take away the stone? Because of the women, because they had earlier seen Jesus in the tomb and so, in order that they may believe that he is risen, they see the tomb empty of the body. The reason for the removal of the stone and for the earthquake was to arouse them from their sleep, since they had come to pour oil on him and this took place at night, and probably some of them had fallen asleep. And why does he say *Do not you be afraid*?[21] First he releases them from their fear, and then he tells them of the resurrection. He says *You* to show them great honour, and also to indicate that final punishment awaits those who had dared to do as the others had done, unless they repent. 'It is not for *you* to fear', he is saying, but for those who crucified him. So having freed them from fear both by his words and by his appearance (for his appearance was bright, as befits one who bears such good news), he went on to say *I know that you are looking for Jesus who was crucified*, not being ashamed to speak of him as crucified, for this is the most important part of his good news. *He has been raised*. How is this known? *As he said*. 'So if you do not believe me,' he means, 'remember his words, and then you will not disbelieve even me.' And he has another proof to offer: *Come, see the place where he lay*.[22] That was why he removed the stone: so that they would later be able to see the proof. *'And tell his disciples*[23] *that they will see him in Galilee.'* Thus he is preparing them to take to others the good news that above all had led them to believe. He did well to say in Galilee, relieving them of anxiety and danger, so that their faith might not be disturbed by fear. *So they left the tomb quickly with fear and great joy.*[24] Why was this? They had seen an amazing and wonderful thing, an empty tomb where earlier they had seen a corpse. So he led them to look, that they might be witnesses both of the tomb and of the resurrection. And they realised that nobody could have taken him, with so many soldiers sitting nearby: only he can have raised himself. So they rejoice and are amazed, and they receive their reward for remaining with him for so long, being the first to see, and to announce the good news, both of what they had heard and of what they had seen.

And as they went out full of fear and joy, behold, *Jesus met them and said, 'Greetings!' And they . . . took hold of his feet,* and running towards him with their joy overflowing they received through touch as well a certain proof of the resurrection, *and worshipped him.*[25] And so what did he say? *Do not be afraid,* and then he too casts out their fear, making the way ready for faith: *go and tell my brothers to go to Galilee: there they will see me.*[26] See how even he sends the good news to his disciples through these women, doing honour to the sex that was most dishonoured, as I have often said,[27] and leading them to hope for good things. (Saint John Chrysostom)[28]

4. The Paschal Vigil Year B

When the sabbath was over, Mary Magdalene and Mary the mother of James, and Salome bought spices, so that they might go and anoint him. And very early on the first day of the week, when the sun had risen, they went to the tomb.[29]

The holy women who had followed the Lord came with

123

spices to the tomb and even after his death they served with gentle care the one they had loved while he was alive. And we who believe in him who died, if we are fragrant with virtue and seek the Lord with good works, also come to his tomb with spices. The fact that the women came to the tomb *very early . . . when the sun had risen,* that is, when the eastern part of the sky was becoming bright, shows that they must have approached from the East, and is a sign of their love and their great eagerness to seek and find the Lord. <>

As they entered the tomb they saw a young man dressed in a white robe sitting on the right side: and they were alarmed.[30] Entering from the East that round structure which had been cut into the rock, they saw an angel sitting on the south side, where the body of Jesus had been laid, for it was on the right, since the body lay with its head to the West and its right side consequently on the North. We must notice why the angel was seen sitting on the right. The left, surely, signifies our present life and the right eternal life, so that it is written *his left hand is under my head and his right hand will embrace me,*[31] since the Church of God has the left hand, that is, prosperity in this present life, beneath her head, keeping it subject out of love for higher things. But the right hand of God embraces her, since all her devotion is consumed with the thought of the eternal happiness he gives. So because our Redeemer had already passed through the corruption of this present life, the angel who came to announce his eternal life fittingly sat on the right side. He appeared in a white robe because he was the herald of our joyous festival, the brightness of his robe being a sign of our rejoicing. Should I say *our* rejoicing or *his*? If I am to tell the truth, I should say *ours* and *his*, since the resurrection of our Redeemer is our festival, since it brought us back to immortality, and is also a festival for the angels, since by calling us to heaven he made up what was lacking in their number.[32] But let us now listen to the words he says to the women as they approach.

Do not be alarmed, he says, as if he said openly 'Let those who do not love the coming of the citizens of heaven be afraid; let those who despair of being admitted to their company because they are weighed down by carnal desires be afraid. But why are you afraid, since you are looking at your own fellow-citizens?' *But go, tell his disciples and Peter that he is going ahead of you to Galilee.*³³ Why is Peter named after the other disciples? If the angel had not mentioned his name, he who had denied his master would not have dared to come with the other disciples. <> We should consider why almighty God, who had decided to set him over the whole Church, allowed him to fear the voice of a servant-girl and to deny him. This was part of the mysterious plan of God's great love, so that he who was to be the shepherd of the Church should learn from his own sin how to show mercy to others. So God first led him to know himself, and then placed him in charge of others, that from his weakness he might know how to tolerate mercifully the weaknesses of others.

The words *he is going ahead of you to Galilee: there you will see him, just as he told you*³⁴ are suitably said of our Saviour, since 'Galilee' means 'completed crossing',³⁵ and he had already completed his crossing from suffering to resurrection, from death to life, from punishment to glory, from corruption to incorruption. He was first seen by his disciples after his resurrection in Galilee because in the future we shall see the glory of his resurrection with joy, provided that we now cross over from sin to the heights³⁶ of virtue. (Saint Bede)³⁷

5. The Paschal Vigil Year C

*But on the first day of the week, at early dawn they came to the tomb, taking the spices that they had prepared.*³⁸

The first day of the week <> is called the Lord's day in Christian tradition because of the Lord's resurrection. The fact that the women came so early shows us the intensity of their love which impelled them to seek and find the Lord, but according to the mystical interpretation it teaches us that we should come to the most holy body of the Lord with the light shining on our faces and the darkness of sin cleared away. That venerable sepulchre was a sign of the altar of the Lord on which the mysteries of his body and blood are celebrated. So the custom of the church is that the mysteries should be consecrated not on silk or coloured cloth but on pure linen like that in which Joseph wound him. As he gave up his true earthly and mortal nature to death for us, so we, in commemoration of that awesome and venerable mystery, place on the altar pure white linen grown from seed in the earth and prepared as if by many kinds of mortification.[39] The spices that the women bring signify the fragrance of the virtues and the sweetness of the prayers with which we must approach the altar. So John in his Apocalypse, having described bowls full of incense in the hands of the angels, that is, pure consciences in the hearts of the elect, added by way of explanation *which are the prayers of the saints.*[40]

They found the stone rolled away from the tomb.[41] <> According to the mystical interpretation, the rolling away of the stone signifies the unlocking of mysteries which had been concealed beneath the literal sense of scripture, for the Law was written on stone. When the covering of the Law is removed, the dead body of the Lord is not discovered: it is his living body that is proclaimed, for even if *we have known Christ after the flesh,*[42] that does yet not mean that we truly know him.

While they were perplexed about this, suddenly two men in dazzling clothes stood beside them.[43] They were perplexed in their minds, both because they were astonished to find that such a huge stone had been rolled away, and also because they were grieved that they could not find the body that they held in such great veneration. But just as angels came and ministered to the Lord in the desert as soon as his victory over temptation was won,[44] so when the same Saviour has suffered in the flesh, having struggled with death and conquered it, angels come to make known the glory of his triumph not only with consoling words but by the brightness of their garments. And as we read that angels were beside the body of the Saviour in the tomb, so we should believe that angels are present at the moment of consecration when the mysteries of his most holy body are celebrated: that is why the Apostle commands that women should be veiled in church *because of the angels*.[45]

The women were terrified and bowed their faces to the ground, but the men said to them, 'Why do you look for the living among the dead? He is not here, but has risen'.[46] <> We should follow the example of these holy women whenever we come to church or approach the heavenly mysteries, and enter with great humility and reverence, both because of the angelic powers who are present and from reverence for the holy sacrifice. In the sight of the angels we bow our faces to the ground since, when we consider the eternal joys of the citizens of heaven, we remember that we are *dust and ashes*, as holy Abraham said.[47] And notice that the holy women did not fall to the ground when the angels stood beside them, but are said to have *bowed their faces to the ground*.[48] We do not read that any of the saints fell to the ground in adoration at the time of the Lord's resurrection when they saw either angels or the Lord himself. From this comes the Church's custom that on every Sunday and throughout the fifty days of Easter we do not pray kneeling but with our faces bowed to the ground, both in memory of the Lord's resurrection and in hope of our own.

And returning from the tomb they told all this to the eleven and to all the rest.[49] Just as at the beginning a woman was initiator of sin for a man and a man followed her example, so now she who first tasted death first witnesses the resurrection and, that she may not be blamed among men for unending sin, she who passed on guilt to a man now passes on grace. (Saint Bede)[50]

6. Easter Day

The two were running together, but the other disciple outran Peter and reached the tomb first,[51] but he did not presume to go inside, while Peter came later, and went into the tomb. What does their running mean? Are we to believe that this story, which the evangelist tells with such care, has no mystical meaning? Certainly not. John would not have told us that he arrived first and did not go in if there was no hidden significance in his hesitation. Surely, John signifies the Synagogue[52] and Peter the Church, and it should not surprise us that the younger stands for the Synagogue and the older for the Church since, although the Synagogue came to the worship of God before the Church of the Gentiles, there were Gentiles in the world before there were Jews, as Paul attests when he says *it is not the spiritual that is first, but the physical.*[53] <> They run together because from the beginning to the end Gentiles and Jews have run the same path, even if not with the same understanding.

Synagogue came first to the tomb, but did not go in, because she had received the commandments of the Law and had heard the prophecies of the incarnation and passion of the Lord, but would not believe in him after his death. John saw the linen wrappings lying, but did not go in, because Synagogue knew the mysteries of sacred Scripture but hesitated to believe and so to enter faith in the Lord's passion. Him whom she had long prophesied she saw present and denied: she despised him as a man, but refused to believe in him as God made mortal in the flesh. So she ran faster, but stood uncertain in front of the tomb. *Then Simon Peter came following him, and went into the tomb,*[54] because the Church of the Gentiles came later and knew the *mediator between God and humankind, the man Christ Jesus*[55] dead in the flesh, and believed in him as the living God.

He saw the linen wrappings lying there and the cloth that had been on Jesus' head, not lying with the linen wrappings but rolled up in a place by itself.[56] The fact that the cloth that had been on the Lord's head was not found in the tomb with the linen wrappings means that, as Paul says, *God is the head of Christ*,[57] and the incomprehensible mysteries of his divinity are kept from our feeble understanding, and his power is greater than his creation. Note that the cloth not only lies separately, but rolled up in a place by itself. When linen is rolled up, neither its beginning nor its end can be seen, and so it was fitting that the head-cloth was found to be rolled up, because the divine majesty has neither beginning nor end. <>

Then the other disciple who reached the tomb first, also went in.[58] John followed Peter into the tomb: the one who had arrived first went in last. You should know, brethren, that at the end of the world the Jews too will be joined to those who believe in the Redeemer, as Paul says . . . *until the full number of the Gentiles has come in. And so all Israel will be saved.*[59] John *saw and believed.*[60] What did he believe, brethren? That the Lord whom he was seeking had risen from the dead? Certainly not, because it was still dark at the tomb, and the words that follow prove it *for as yet they did not understand the scripture, that he must rise from the dead.*[61] What did he see, and what did he believe? He saw the linen cloths lying, and he believed what the woman had said, that the Lord had been taken away from the tomb. This should help us to realise the great mystery of God's ways, since he inspires the hearts of the disciples to seek him, and then delays their finding him so that their weak spirits may be purged by suffering, and when they do find him they may cling to him the more strongly the longer it has taken them to find him whom they were seeking. (Pope Saint Gregory the Great)[62]

NOTES

1. John 13:1
2. The word *Pasch* was often used in English in earlier times to refer to what is now usually known as the Passover: the common word *Paschal* derives from it. The

old word has been used in this passage to make Augustine's meaning clearer.
3. Is 53:7
4. Ex 12:22-23
5. Col 1:13
6. Rom 10:4
7. 1 Cor 5:7
8. *Commentary on John* 55, 1-2; *PL* 35, 1784-1785
9. John 19:28
10. 1 Tim 2:5
11. Jer 17:9 (in the Greek and Old Latin versions)
12. cf. John 10:18
13. John 19:30
14. John 19:34
15. Gen 6:16
16. Gen 2:21-22
17. Gen 3:20
18. John 19:41
19. *Commentary on John* 119, 4-120, 5; *PL* 35, 1951-1954
20. Matt 28:2-5
21. Chrysostom points out that the angel explicitly says *you* to the women in the original Greek of the Gospel.
22. Matt 28:6
23. Matt 28:7
24. Matt 28:8
25. Matt 28:9
26. Matt 28:10
27. cf. Chrysostom's commentary on the Gospel of Palm Sunday Year A (above p.121)
28. *Commentary on Matthew* 89, 2-3; *PG* 58, 783-784
29. Mark 16:1-2
30. Mark 16:5
31. Songs 2:6
32. That is, after the number of the angels had been reduced by the fall of Satan and his companions.
33. Mark 16:7

34. Mark 16:7
35. a mistaken interpretation: Galilee probably means 'circle' or 'district'.
36. Galilee, it will be remembered, is surrounded by hills.
37. *Commentary on Mark* 4, 16; *PL* 92, 295-297
38. Luke 24:1
39. The preparation of linen involves harsh treatment of the stalks of the flax-plant.
40. cf Apoc 5:8; 15:7
41. Luke 22:2
42. 2 Cor 5:16
43. Luke 22:4
44. Matt 4:11; Mark 1:13
45. 1 Cor 11:10
46. Luke 24:5
47. Gen 18:27
48 Luke 24:5
49. Luke 24:9
50. *Commentary on Luke* 6, 24; *PL* 92, 622-624
51. John 20:4
52. i.e. the Jewish people. In common with many early Christians, Gregory personifies Synagogue and Church as two women. They are thus depicted in a mosaic of the fifth century in the basilica of Santa Sabina in Rome, which Gregory will have seen often.
53. 1 Cor 15:46
54. John 20:6
55. 1 Tim 2:5
56. John 20:6-7
57. 1 Cor 11:3
58. John 20:8
59. Rom 11:25-26
60. John 20:8
61. John 20:9
62. *Homily 22* (on the Saturday of Easter Week), 2-5; *PL* 76, 1175-1177